the LONG {and short} OF IT

HARPERENTERTAINMENT

The Long (and Short) of It: The Madcap History of the Skirt
is produced by becker&mayer!, Bellevue, Washington.
www.beckermayer.com

FIRST EDITION

Design by Megan Noller Holt
Production coordination by Nick Boone-Lutz
Project management by Kate Perry

ISBN-10: 0-06-121298-9
ISBN-13: 978-0-06-121298-7

07 08 09 10 11   10 9 8 7 6 5 4 3 2 1

the
LONG
{and short}
OF IT

THE MADCAP HISTORY of the SKIRT

by ALI BASYE

HARPERENTERTAINMENT
New York • London • Toronto • Sydney

TABLE OF CONTENTS

The Skirt Tree   6

Introduction: Skirting the Issue   9

1: It's a Wrap   15

2: To Skirt or Not to Skirt   27

3: Doing the Bump   33

4: Big and Blowsy   45

5: Baby Got Back   57

6: Fettered Calves   65

7: Rebels with a Cause   73

8: Crashing Down   85

9: Cold-War Years   93

10: The Birth of Preppy   101

11: Felt Fancy   109

12: The Miniskirt Revolution   119

13: Folk Songs and Flower Dreams   129

14: Pre-Disco Doldrums   137

15: The Sexless Trouser Skirt   147

16: The Twenty-first Century   157

17: The Thigh's the Limit   167

Conclusion: Wrapping Things Up   173

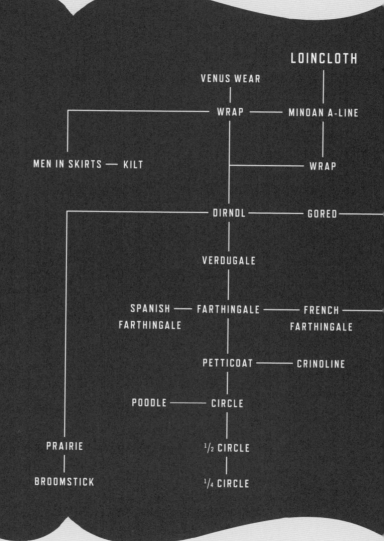

LOINCLOTH

VENUS WEAR

WRAP —— MINOAN A-LINE

WRAP

MEN IN SKIRTS — KILT

DIRNDL —— GORED

VERDUGALE

SPANISH —— FARTHINGALE —— FRENCH
FARTHINGALE   FARTHINGALE

PETTICOAT —— CRINOLINE

POODLE —— CIRCLE

PRAIRIE

BROOMSTICK

$1/2$ CIRCLE

$1/4$ CIRCLE

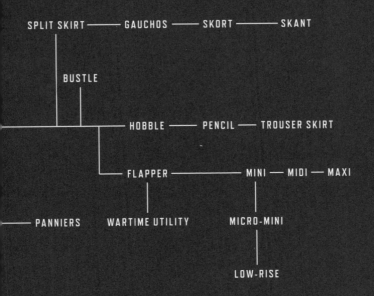

SPLIT SKIRT —— GAUCHOS —— SKORT —— SKANT

BUSTLE

HOBBLE —— PENCIL —— TROUSER SKIRT

FLAPPER —————————— MINI — MIDI — MAXI

PANNIERS   WARTIME UTILITY   MICRO-MINI

LOW-RISE

the **SKIRT TREE**

"A skirt is no obstacle to extemporaneous sex, but it is physically impossible to make love to a girl while she is wearing trousers."

◇◇◇

HELEN LAWRENSON,
ribald American writer

SKIRTING THE ISSUE

No garment is as significant in the evolution of clothing and in determining gender roles as the skirt. From its simple beginnings as a unisex body wrap to its bold march forward as a feminist statement, the skirt has had a perilous journey—one day subject to accolades, the next, ridicule, and another, coming under fire before the Supreme Court. As an art form or utilitarian wear, the cultural and social significance of the skirt through the ages is far grander than merely serving as an article of clothing.

As the world's original garment, the skirt started out humbly enough as a simple wrap or loincloth, which served merely to protect goods from sunburn, frostbite, and the occasional randy Neanderthal with a roving eye. In its early days, it was good enough for everybody: male and female, rich and poor. But around the 1100s men's skirts began inching higher till their hose transformed into trousers and, ultimately, pants. Skirts, no longer worn by all, became associated with weakness and feminity.

as the hemline turns

The use of the word "skirt" changed with its styles and with women's place in society. The first usage to describe the garment was a derivative of either the Swedish *skjorta*, the Danish and Norwegian *skjorte*, or an Old Norse word, *skyrta*, still used in Iceland, all of which translate to "shirt." The origin's exact definition is unclear, but it is likely that the variation on the word came about to differentiate between the top and bottom halves of the long shirts worn by peasants in parts of northern Europe.

According to the *Dictionary of Contemporary English*, the Middle English word "skirt" first appeared around 1300 to define "the part of a dress or similar garment that extends downward from the waist; (hence) a one-piece garment extending downward from the waist, worn especially by women and girls."

Around the fifteenth century, "skirt" appeared as a noun meaning "border," as in "The best tailors were found on the outskirts of town," and by the seventeenth century the word was used as a verb meaning "to avoid," as in "The women skirted past the group of leering men on the corner."

Around 1560, "skirt" became synonymous for "women as a group," as in "round up the skirts, the knights are in town for a party." This usage came back into play in the early twentieth century when the British slang "a bit of skirt" came to crudely refer to an attractive woman, reducing a female down to her identifying garment—and to what lay beneath it. In 1942, "skirt chaser" came to describe the scurrilous man who couldn't get enough of the ladies.

No matter how you wear it or how you say it, there's no denying the skirt's power to seduce, bewilder, mortify, and enchant, and over the years the skirt has seen and done it all. Ronald Knox, a twentieth-century English theologian and crime writer, once said, "A good sermon should be like a woman's skirt: short enough to rouse the interest, but long enough to cover the essentials." Hopefully, *The Long (and Short) of It* does both.

THE FIRST LADIES OF SKIRTS

Beside every powerful man is an even stronger lady and, in some cases, a well-attired one at that. Over the past 200-some years, America's First Ladies have proved to be some of the country's greatest fashion influences.

MARTHA WASHINGTON: Hubby George was an admitted clotheshorse and dressed all the members of his family formally to complement his dapper eighteenth-century wardrobe, Martha and her hoopskirts included.

DOLLEY MADISON: She launched the tradition of throwing a formal inaugural reception and ball, encouraging early Philadelphians to ditch the Quaker duds and bust out their finery. The Empire waist was the look, and the spirited First Lady amassed a wardrobe of these evening dresses and ball gowns.

MARY TODD LINCOLN: The physical and spiritual opposite of her morose husband, the elegant Mary caught flak in the press for her highfalutin tastes and extravagant spending, including cage crinolines and multitiered ruffled top skirts.

EDITH ROOSEVELT: Teddy's better half was a thrifty one: In a move that was very *Pretty in Pink*, she used the skirt from one dress and the bodice from another to create her own budget-friendly inaugural gown.

MAMIE EISENHOWER: This fashion plate had the good luck to land in the White House just before Christian Dior launched his "New Look," a collection that included full skirts and petticoats. Mamie adored them and bought mountains of the things.

JACQUELINE KENNEDY: Jackie remains the quintessential First Lady of fashion. She designed her own white satin strapless inaugural gown and promoted several American designers, in particular Oleg Cassini, who dressed her in many above-the-knee skirts.

NANCY REAGAN: As a size-four former Hollywood starlet, Nancy never missed an opportunity to pile on the bling and show a little leg in her midi skirts. Nancy caused a stir for her habit of "borrowing" couture that often didn't find its way home.

BARBARA BUSH: A champion of designer Arnold Scassi, Babs is often credited with single-handedly bringing costume jewelry back into vogue in the late 80s, but her modest skirts left much to be desired.

"That skirt is to die for."

◇◇◇

DR. OLGA SOFFER,

archaeologist, commenting on a string skirt worn by an
Upper Paleolithic woman 25,000 years ago

CHAPTER 1

IT'S A WRAP

Venus Vogue

Never underestimate the power of a woman and her wardrobe. A century ago, when the famous Venus figurines—27,000-year-old topless statuettes of Rubenesque female bodies—were discovered in what is now eastern Europe, scientists were so obsessed with analyzing what they were convinced was prehistoric erotica that they overlooked the obvious: These Ice Age babes were trekking the tundra in rather stylish, low-slung, frayed skirts, some of which featured detailed fringe, twisted strings, and curiously tapered, tailcoat-like backsides. Sewn with delicate woven cloth, the skirts were paired with strapless bandeaux (essentially cupless bras), belts, multiple bracelets, and jaunty haberdashery. Venus Wear, it appears, was very Madonna, circa "Like a Virgin."

What a revelation! Ancient women weren't dragged around caves by their hair—they were too busy sewing coordinates and matching skirt sets. In fact, if any clubbing was going on, it appears it was down at the Bedrock Discothèque, à la *The Flintstones*. (Eat your heart out, Wilma: Your poorly cut, plain white shift has been *served*.) These skirts, woven from plant fibers and cut and stitched to fit, were the anchor of any self-respecting cavewoman's wardrobe. Fashion was officially invented.

not so fast...

Despite the textile innovations indicated on the Venus figurines, archaeological evidence shows other cultures of the same era lacked the style savvy of these ancient Material Girls. Elsewhere on the old continent, fashion-challenged Cro-Magnons utilized animal skin as an evergreen fashion staple, often with the fur left on in a clumsy cut that was more ghetto than Gucci. Silk and cotton were still a long time coming, so B.C. women worked it with cumbersome felt, woven wool, or rough linen. And this look stuck. (Fast forward 23,000 years to the first century B.C., and Cleopatra couldn't put together something more tailored than a belted toga?)

In ancient Mesopotamia from 3500 to 250 B.C., draping was all the rage. To craft the basic skirt, both women and men would take a square, rectangle, or semicircular piece of wool

fur loincloth

or linen, give it the old one-two wraparound, pin it with a fibula (a.k.a. a brooch), and shout out the Sumerian equivalent of "Showtime!" Couture it was not. If the fabric was long enough, the ends were slipped up and under a belt and over one shoulder, creating what we know as a Roman toga; otherwise the gals went topless. The variations on the drape of these pieces created distinctive styles characteristic of particular cultures.

Across many societies for several millennia, unisex skirt lengths varied according to class: Servants and soldiers wore shorter lengths; royalty and deities flaunted their wealth by wearing them longer. Even after woven fabric supplemented sheepskin and other furs, the cloth of all castes was often deliberately fringed at the hem or constructed to simulate the tufts of wool on the fleece.

For instance, in ancient Egypt during that same era, guys wore a wrapped kilt called a *schenti* or *kalasiris*, likely made out of linen or wool, while slaves wore a lone, shabby loincloth. Lower-class Egyptian women such as slaves, musicians, dancers, and acrobats wore draped skirts and worked topless.

In Greece, the citizens' decadence and debauchery did not extend to their costumes; in terms of clothing they were the Gap of the ancient world. For both genders, a simply designed but nicely embellished skirt was the foundation piece. Greek women were gifted weavers with a talent for embroidery, dyeing, and pleating, and they used their skills to sex up their uncomplicated and simple wardrobes with geometric designs and decorative elements. Ancient Olympians wore a small, wrapped loincloth, which was quickly abandoned altogether in favor of competing in the buff. Given today's squeamish reactions to wardrobe malfunctions, this noble tradition is sadly no longer practiced.

For thousands of years, the average tribe of the Western world wore unadorned loincloth-style skirts, but there are notable exceptions elsewhere in the world. The ancient Chinese, for example, were rocking richly colored, elaborate silks and other embroidered fabrics as early as 6000 B.C., long before Westerners caught on to advancements in textile design. During the Xia dynasty (2100 to 1800 B.C.), men and women wore a decoratively pattered *yi*, a long jacket, paired with a *chang*, a long, loose straight skirt. Other artifacts show matching silk-blouse-and-skirt sets, with material for the skirt folded into as many as ten widths of the expensive fabric, so that the skirt created a rippling effect when a woman walked in it. In the Tang dynasty (A.D. 618–907), a streamer with a jade ornament attached to the end ran down the front of long skirts, to serve as a weight, preventing the fabric from fluttering up in the wind and possibly exposing an ankle, which could be detrimental to the dignity of an upstart Chinese debutante.

YOU *CAN* TAKE IT WITH YOU.
ANCIENT FASHIONISTA:
THE ORIGINAL CORPSE BRIDE

Death is scary. It's frightening to think of what awaits us in
the afterlife, and no one was more afraid than Madame Xiin
Zhui, the Marquise of Dai in China. Never one to be caught
improperly attired, this lady of the Han dynasty was entombed
upon her death 2,100 years ago with more than 100 articles
of clothing, including skirts, gowns, and, oddly, mittens, to
ensure her stay in the next world was a warm and fashionable
one. Mummified in eighteen layers of silk and buried in four
successive caskets surrounded by 5,000 kilos of charcoal, when
exhumed in the 1970s, Madame Zhui's hair was still black, her
skin youthfully supple, and her limbs pliable. Alas, the scientist
who unearthed her was not, as this Sleeping Beauty might have
hoped, Prince Charming—and Madame remained a corpse.

yi and chang

minoan
tiered a-line

forever a-line

Far across the continent on Crete, Neolithic Minoans (2600–1450 B.C.) carried on the traditions of their distant Venus sisters' variations on the basic skirt, but raised them one by designing the classic A-line skirt. From the ruins of palaces and mountains of archaeological records, we know the Minoan culture distinguished itself as a peaceful, non-warring society that worshiped females; in fact, its rulers were quite likely women. No wonder the fitted A-line, highly flattering and comfortable on every female figure, was the skirt *du jour*.

In this matriarchal fashion capital, the palace at Knossos was built and held the first fashion *atelier*, complete with a spinning and weaving shop and statuettes that—who knows?—may have been dressmakers' dummies. Either way, technical garment construction as we know it today was established in this ancient workshop.

Minoan skirts were some of the chicest garments of the primordial world. Floor-length and bell-shaped, their skirts of dyed linen or wool were crafted in three different styles: the aforementioned smooth A-line, fitted at the waist and flaring gently to the ground; one made of a series of tiered, flounced ruffles, often with an elaborate apron-like panel covering the front of the hips; and a third whose specific cut is unknown, possibly designed like the ruffled skirt, but with the tiers falling in either a V-shape, or cut into elegant, loose, wide-leg ruffled trousers. (There are no existing remains of these skirts, merely art and other artifacts on which to speculate.) As Minoan designs evolved, the skirts became increasingly colorful and elaborate, with added embroidery and other decorations, like checkerboard pleats and ruffles.

Based on statuettes and paintings, archaeologists have conjectured that Minoan skirts were worn over hoops of rushes, wood, or metal, in what would have been the earliest boned crinoline. Whether this guess is accurate—would a society ruled by power babes *really* have worn hoopskirts?— the hoops were summarily ditched for a looser, hippie-chick look, completed with tightly laced, full-breast-baring bodices, open-toed sandals, and shawls.

Here lies the murky area of fashion history: Minoan women's costume—billowing, tiered skirts, corsets, and elaborate embroidery, jewelry, color, and decoration— was essentially a sexy forerunner of high-court fashion of the Renaissance, nearly two millennia later. So what happened to skirts in between those years? A likely theory is that around 1400 B.C., when the female-friendly Minoan civiliza- tion was wiped out—most likely by a volcanic eruption or tsunamis—its textile innovations and advances in fashion were buried in the rubble. Without the benefit of ever learning the skills of Crete's seamstresses, women's fashion elsewhere around the globe devolved, and drab drapery once again dominated. From the third century through the years leading up to the Renaissance, the style—if you could call it that—was a colorless tunic paired with a floor-length dirndl, a full skirt with a gathered waistband, less fitted and more one-note than anything the Minoans ever crafted. It was a millennium of Dowdy Debbies. Maybe the 2,000 years of zero-tolerance patriarchal rule that followed the footloose, fashionable spirit of the Minoans had something to do with it. Take away a woman's self-esteem and she becomes . . . frumpy. In fact, the men of the Middle Ages were the real fashion plates, while women suffered their repression in those dang dirndls. Perhaps men understood that with a little fashion freedom, women might get assertive enough to do something daring like, you know, try to vote or get an education.

"All this I see; and I see that
the fashion wears out
more apparel than the man.
But art thou thyself
giddy with the fashion too, that
thou hast shifted out
of thy tale into telling me of
the fashion?"

◇◇◇

WILLIAM SHAKESPEARE,
Much Ado About Nothing, Act III, Scene III

CHAPTER 2

TO SKIRT OR NOT TO SKIRT

orget the Inquisition and the Crusades. The real crime of the Middle Ages was committed when ruling knights renounced skirts and slid into their first pair of tight, silky, knee-length breeches. After that, shapely legs were regarded as a sign of virile masculinity, and skirtwearers (i.e., the ladies) were promptly delegated to the bottom of the pecking order. The social implications were swift and lasting: No longer in a position to call the shots, twelfth-century women were forbidden, by law and religion, to follow suit. Stuck in long, miserable, dowdy dirndls, they had to bat their eyes and compliment the bombastic buffoons strutting about the castle in tights, garters, and stockings, under what were becoming alarmingly short skirts.

Historians claim the English Plantagenet era (1154–1485) inspired all things elegant and long, like close-fitting tights,

GREAT MEN
IN TIGHTS

William Shakespeare
Robin Hood
King Arthur
Superman
Mikhail Baryshnikov
Prince
Lance Armstrong
Alex Rodriguez

revealing long, strong legs. Before men adopted legged undergarments, their doublets (padded shirts with a skirted bottom) hovered safely at knee-length. But once knights donned the new close-fitting breeches that revealed their legs, men's skirts gradually began creeping to exhibitionist heights. By 1485, a codpiece was essential—ordered by clerics, no less—to keep twigs and berries out of sight.

Trunk hose were actually two separate fitted leg sleeves that fastened to the underside of a doublet with garter-like fasteners in a kind of medieval *Rocky Horror Picture Show* ensemble. Underwear wasn't in vogue (nor was *bathing*), and these guys were just sitting all over the place in long shirts and garters. *Ew.*

In the early part of the last millennium, cool knights in tights were the Fonzies of the medieval world. Kings and their subjects paid homage by copying the tight, sexy look and air-jousting in front of the mirrors in their bedrooms. Men really got into hose, wearing them in contrasting colors or decorated in vertical stripes, all through the early 1600s. In fact, with their corsets, garters, stockings, hose, wigs, and the like, these foppish fashion hounds were just as, if not more so, conscious of clothing as their lady friends were. It's as if every Hamlet suddenly had his own Fab Five, putting on a countrywide *Queer Eye for the Medieval Guy*. (The two-stocking thing explains why we say "pair of pants" for a single garment. Until the late sixteenth century, leg coverings were two separate pieces. At the time, calling them a "pair" made sense, and it stuck.)

Later the breeches and hose became one garment, like very tight trousers. As this garment got looser, the trunk hose

got shorter and stockings kept the calves warm. Eventually, trousers grew longer and stockings shorter and, *voilà*, pants, first as pantaloon breeches in the seventeenth century and later as tight-fitting trousers in the eighteenth century.

These newfangled pants revolutionized fashion. Most men no longer wore skirts because, seriously, it's tough to ride a horse in one. Plus, explorers of the New World needed freedom to fell trees and slaughter native tribes without the fear they'd tear their hose. Save the blessed Scots, when men switched to pants, they never looked back.

With short skirts and tights deemed too risqué for women, medieval gals held their own in increasingly cumbersome and ever heavier long skirts. As men's skirts shrunk, ladies' skirts became more elaborate, and women learned to employ other tools of seduction in order to get a leg up in the patriarchal world. Tiny slippers peeked from lacy hemlines, underskirts mysteriously rustled, fans slipped from hidden skirt pockets to mask batting eyes. Vying for attention, skirt shapes frequently expanded up and out, morphing into grander architectural wonders to brush the legs of potential suitors. Mandatory long skirts—with all their material and various contraptions— seemed to keep women (literally) in their place, but they sure as hell weren't going to keep them from competing in the battle of the sexes.

DIVINITY IN DRAG

Though there's much rabble-rousing among a faction of today's fundamentalists to get women back in skirts (and barefoot and breeding, no doubt), the garment has a sacred history pious males should heed and consider embracing the skirt for themselves. From the first fig-leaf loincloth to chic belted wraps, God, Adam, Jesus, and all holy brethren in between walked the ancient world in skirts. The King James and Revised Standard Bibles both cite early Jews wearing "aprons." *The Living Bible* says Adam and Eve covered "themselves around the hips," while the *New American Standard Bible* modestly refers to "loin coverings." *The Modern Language* edition mentions "skirts" in various cryptic references: "And it came to pass afterward that David's heart smote him, because he had cut off Saul's skirt" (1 Samuel 24:5), and "A man shall not take his father's wife, nor discover his father's skirt" (Deuteronomy 22:30). So this we know: The dames *and* dudes were in skirts. A few choice nuggets shed light on why strict religions want modern women in skirts:

"The woman shall not wear that which pertaineth unto a man, neither shall a man put on a woman's garment: for all that do so are abomination unto the Lord thy God." —*Deuteronomy 22:5*

"Those women who imitate the appearance of men, (including physical appearance and dress), incur the wrath of Allah Ta'aala." —Muhammad Bukhari, author of *Hadith*, ancient Muslim traditions, ninth century A.D.

"Her filthiness is in her skirts." —*Lamentations 1:9*

"In like manner also, that women adorn themselves in modest apparel, with shamefacedness and sobriety." —*1 Timothy 2:9*

"Your dresses should
be tight enough
to show you're a woman
and loose enough
to show you're a lady."

✧✧✧

EDITH HEAD,
eight-time Oscar-winning Hollywood
costume designer

CHAPTER 3

DOING THE BUMP

farthingales, bum rolls, and panniers

By the Middle Ages, it was all too clear where women stood in the world, and couturiers, kowtowing to the whims of lords and the misguided delusions of ladies, found myriad ways to keep the increasingly uppity broads down. They crafted binding support garments that, by emphasizing hips, busts, or butts, inhibited unimportant stuff, like walking, breathing, and sitting. Even the discovery of blood circulation in 1628 didn't end the suffering and injuries to women's bodies, although it did kindle widespread fears of vampires. (Check out those high-neck ruffled collars!)

bound to please

A primitive version of the hoopskirt may have been seen first in Crete as long ago as 2000 B.C., but an updated version, the farthingale, featuring bigger hoops and tighter bindings, was shuffled out at the Spanish court in 1468. Originally called a *verdugale* (from the Spanish word *verdugo*, for green wood) before the British butchered the pronunciation, the cone-shaped, willow-cane contraption was sewn directly into beautiful fabric and served as a visible design element, as the brocade top skirts were often lifted and pinned in areas to flaunt the undergarment's architecture. Though Catalonian bad girls clung to this sixteenth-century equivalent of showing your bra strap, elsewhere the hoops were gravity-defying support systems built separately from the fabric.

Inspired by the style of the continent-trotting Spanish princess Catherine of Aragon, ladies across Europe scrambled to get their bodies into the unwieldy device, and as the skirt crossed borders, spreading like the Black Plague, it grew in name and shape. A bell-shaped farthingale (similar to the style worn by our old friends, the Minoans) was popular throughout Europe. The shape especially complemented the Tudor style of the mid-sixteenth century: a stiff conical skirt, like an angel atop a Christmas tree, paired with a tight bodice and a high, starched, ruffle collar.

The French so preferred a wide and narrow farthingale—imagine two invisible strings holding either sides of the skirt out above the hips—that it is called the French farthingale. The version that really took off, though, is the wheel,

farthingale

or drum, farthingale. It was more circular, like a drum shape, and grew ever more wide—imagine wearing a round, tiered birthday cake or a starched tutu underneath an outer skirt. The waistband was heavily gathered to keep the look smooth and tidy, and an ellipse-shaped miniskirt was laid atop to hide the gathers. (For those of you keeping track, that's now *four* skirts these gals were wearing: a farthingale, an underskirt, an outer skirt, and a top miniskirt.) Made of cane or whalebone hoops stacked the same circumference from top to bottom, the grand device inspired early Renaissance fashion victims to compete and scheme to have the widest hoops at the ball. Some accounts report farthingales five feet wide—as wide as the average lady was tall! To boot—or should we say, to boo-*tay*—now a bum roll was added to better support the shape and maintain a smooth line on the fast growing skirts.

The bum roll, if you haven't had the pleasure of wearing one yourself, is a large donut-shaped mass of fabric stuffed and stitched on to the top hoop of the farthingale, which ran the circumference of the device. Its purpose was to add more width to the hips while keeping the skirt's drape smooth, the motion swishy, and the appearance of floating just above the ground. (One has to imagine it also added a little kick to the can, making for memorable exits.)

Pair the bum roll with the French farthingale, and you've got that serving-tray-around-the-hips look favored

MY FUNNY VALENTINE

One of history's great skirt fables centers around Queen Marguerite de Valois (1552–1615) of Navarre, Spain, and the thirty-four pockets she supposedly sewed into the lining of her gargantuan hoopskirt. Legend has it that these macabre pockets were not reserved for condoms, lipstick, or breath mints, but held the embalmed hearts of her thirty-four successive sweethearts, with each heart sealed in a separate box. Her family beheaded those who volunteered—or were personally selected—to sate her voracious sexual appetite, thus Marguerite's nickname: the Queen of Hearts. This oft-repeated "strange-but-true" tale is too good to be true: Queen Marguerite took many lovers, but we can presume the only thing left behind on her skirts was a little DNA from the male persuasion, not disembodied organs.

bum roll

by Queen Elizabeth I. The width of the hips was so dispro-
portionate that heads were styled with towering bouffants,
and high-standing collars and puffs of fabric on the
shoulders of long sleeves offered balanced, height-weight-
proportionate dimensions.

For a while things calmed down and hoops stopped
growing, though hips remained heavily padded, and waists
and breasts were cinched tighter than ever. During the
seventeenth century, "false rumps," a variation on the bum
roll, and other hip pads were stuffed with cork or other
cushioning materials to create even grander booty swish.
Top skirts now featured an always-practical train, and
underskirts peeked out several inches below the hem of the
outer skirt. Skirts grew increasingly extravagant, with
festively patterned fabrics festooned with ribbons, tassels,
flowers, and layers of draped, tucked, tiered, cinched, and
puffed draperies. But progression was nigh: Hems were
raised just a *teensy* bit, and at the start of the 1700s, a randy
spot of ankle could finally be glimpsed.

basket cases

The 1700s were not a hallmark century for the evolution of
the skirt. The construction of dresses, rather than a skirt and
bodice sewn together, was all the rage, as were Empire
waistlines and sack dresses. Originating in France, *sacque*

SIXTEENTH-CENTURY BEAUTY TIPS

Let's just get it right out in the open: These broads didn't bathe. Ever! Believing that water was dangerous for the skin, sixteenth-century ladies covered bodily soil and dirt with thick, pasty applications of cosmetics.

Italy's Catherine de Medici was quite the glamourpuss. A sixteenth-century cosmetics guinea pig, she tried any new formula her "doctors" invented. White lead, for a pale complexion, was popular, with the day's application layered atop the one from the night before. Mercury sublimate was another must-have for "healing" rough skin and blemishes. How distressing it must have been to continually mask pus-filled open sores and the large, rotting gray patches that kept appearing from this mixture. But no worries: A cure-all paste of mercury, alum, honey, and eggshells reportedly freshened up any complexion.

Catherine's stepdaughter, Queen Elizabeth I, became the century's quintessential cosmetic trendsetter, partly because she was no oil painting herself. Upping the ante on her stepmom's regime, Elizabeth packed on mercuric sulfide for rosy lips and cheeks, penciled in veins, and applied black velvet spots (as beauty marks) to accentuate her poison-steeped pale skin. The more paste she applied, the more ravaged her skin became, spurring Liz to wear even heavier coats of toxicant. To suit the style, hairline and eyebrows were heavily plucked, and wigs were a necessity.

The advent of perfume the following century was a blessing. Ungodly b.o. was masked with perfumed pomanders and purses fastened to belts and neck chains, and aromatic lozenges gamely fought foul breath. By the eighteenth century, wash balls— a blend of rice powder, flour, starch, white lead, and oris root— were used before the invention of soap. It was a start.

dresses were nothing less than unflattering, with loose trains free-falling down the back, masking the waist and behind. The sack dress morphed into the softer *gown à la Français*— a richly decorated dress with a close-fitting bodice, opening in front with a V-shaped piece of ornamental cloth in the front and two large double pleats falling in the back—and then into the even more relaxed *gown à l'Anglaise*—a gown without a stiff boned bodice, with a long point reaching down the middle of the back to below the waist.

It was under these loose sack skirts that *panniers* picked up where the French farthingale left off. On formal occasions, these metal hoops were stacked or fitted atop one another, so they resembled a futuristic spider ready to pounce upon a basketball-sized fly lurking under the petticoat folds. Ladies found climbing into carriages and entering theater boxes a total drag, not to mention the embarrassment caused by squeaky pannier hinges. (Nothing says *passé* like a rusty skirt). The size of the pannier decreased decade by decade and in the 1760s these devices were reduced to basket panniers—individual midsized metal halfbaskets attached to the sides of the hips—until they were replaced altogether by numerous heavily starched underskirts.

Marie Antoinette (1755–1793), an ostentatious fashion victim if ever there was one, loathed binding corsets and panniers. This queen always got what she wanted (at least until the bitter end), so daytime hoops were shepherded out during her reign, and women of the court wore soft white skirts that fell in elegant pleats. Ironically, Marie's increasingly simplistic skirt preferences were very bourgeois-friendly. The informal peasant style was in full swing at the end of the eighteenth century, right in time for the French Revolution—and the doomed queen's beheading for, natch, extravagance.

"Since hoops came into fashion, cases of injury and death from the burning of clothes have been much more common and much attention has been lately directed to them."

◇◇◇

THE ALEXANDRA MAGAZINE,
a Victorian feminist publication, 1864

CHAPTER 4

BIG AND BLOWSY

withering waifs and the nineteenth-century romantics

wo opposing spirits clashed in the nineteenth century: industrialism and Romanticism. What resulted was a series of well-tailored fainting spells. The moneyed folks of the early nineteenth century were quite world-weary and prone to collapse, fret, or take to bed at the errant drop of a handkerchief. Poets such as Lord Byron, Shelley, and Keats reflected the language of these "Romantics"—idealistic, fatigued martyrs overburdened with the Big Issues concerning humanity. The fashion, especially that of women, was reflective of these overall sentiments, and garments were given historical flourishes, such as poufy sleeves, ruffled collars inspired by the Tudors, and mountains of rustling petticoats, making a simple stroll to the front gate a melodramatic exercise that would have made the Brontës proud.

empire dress

First featured on dresses introduced in Europe in the late eighteenth-century, the gentle Empire-style waistline gathered under the bust. It was still the fashionable costume in the beginning of the nineteenth century, when Josephine Bonaparte wore it and sustained its popularity. Empire dresses and what were called round skirts were split at the front to display elaborate petticoats, worn not as an undergarment but a visible underskirt. Women now had the freedom needed to move their legs and run with a lover in slow motion through fields of wildflowers. As the public grew ever more genteel, though, women's wardrobes evolved into a more prim and sentimental style. Waistlines dropped back to the waist, and sleeves were set so low on the shoulder that women couldn't possibly lift their arms above their heads—no wonder they were always flinging themselves onto chaises and bursting into tears. For these morose martyrs, it was highly unfashionable to look healthy; better to appear exhausted or full of despair, with ashen skin and dark circles under the eyes. To stay *au courant*, gals used paling, bluish cosmetics to achieve these woeful marks of ennui.

When ladies did manage to climb down off their crosses and into their clothes, the definitive garment was the crinoline petticoat. Woven of linen and horsehair, the 1830s crinoline was like the flouncing peasant-style under-skirt we call a crinoline today and not the caged and hooped

FASHION MAGAZINES

Before there was American *Vogue* there was the British *Ladies'
Mercury* in 1693. For the first time women of all social classes
could see the Parisian fashion of the day, while devouring a mix
of lifestyle articles about love, marriage, and manners. When
Gentleman's Magazine was founded in England in 1731, it
coined the word *magazine*, adopted by the public ever since.
In 1785, *Cabinet des Modes* presented the first colored
illustrations and proposed that fashion integrate all topics,
including furniture, interior décor, coaches, and jewelry,
becoming the first lifestyle magazine along the lines of today's
Town & Country. Germany's *Journal des Luxus und der Moden*
included fashion plates drawn by Gravelot and Moreau le
Jeune. At the dawn of the Victorian era, *Godey's Lady's Book*
(1830) and *Peterson's Magazine* (1842) were the definitive
must-reads for any self-respecting fashionista. And in 1858,
the *Englishwoman's Domestic Magazine* offered a pattern
service to readers that delivered stylish paper dress patterns
by mail order, allowing women to knock off the fashions
featured in its pages.

contraptions that were given the same name just a few decades later in the century. By the 1840s, oversized, dramatic ruffles were added to the already full skirts, some made with accordion, organ, or flat pleating, making them appear even broader and more overwhelming. The top skirts also grew in size, and up to twelve crinolines, even in the sweltering days of summer, were necessary to get that oh-so-emotionally fatigued look.

nineteenth-century crinoline

a fashion boon: sweatshops!

As well-to-do women of the Romantic era were whiling the days away, the rest of the free world was relishing the new industrial era—or, as was more often the case, toiling away one's health in it. Both England's and the New World's "needle trades"—textile and fashion industries—were thriving, and women were readily employed (and exploited) in cramped and dangerous conditions, working arduously ten or twelve hours a day, six or seven days a week.

The first department stores opened in the mid-nineteenth century, where the rich and not-so-rich could shop side by side for entire outfits, fabric, and accessories, under one roof. In Paris, though, true fashionistas avoided these *magasins* like the plague, and the dressmaker became one of the more prestigious careers of the era. To further crumble visible distinctions between the classes, fashion magazines became available to all, bringing the latest styles to servants, housewives, and muckety-mucks. In 1846, Isaac Singer invented the sewing machine, which was soon followed by garment steamers, and knitting and button machines. Ready-to-wear had arrived, and ladies scrambled to get their hands on it. Fashion was no longer reserved for royalty and aristocracy, and old-money broads had to find a way to prove their exclusivity.

THE BIRTH OF COUTURE: THE HOUSES OF WORTH AND DOUCET

Truly chic French women wouldn't be caught shopping in department stores. They visited couturiers—private dressmakers—and, if they were very wealthy, the famous House of Worth on rue de la Paix. Universally considered the founder of *haute couture,* Charles Frederick Worth (1826–1895) crafted garments that were considered high art at the height of the Industrial Revolution. Clients such as the Empress Eugénie, Napoleon III's wife, and Austria's Princess Pauline von Metternich battled it out for his handmade-to-fit garments. He is also credited with introducing, and later banishing, the crinoline and the bustle.

Worth's contemporary, Jacques Doucet (1853–1929), was the other half of the city's elite couturiers. Doucet wisely sought out wealthy women who were not old-money rich. In his Parisian shop, actresses and mistresses mingled with princesses and society ladies from America and Europe. Of note, he employed and mentored Paul Poiret and Madeleine Vionnet, who became renowned designers in their own right.

Together Worth and Doucet made legendary contributions to the fashion industry, establishing the same techniques and patterns used today by *couture* designers such as John Galliano, Karl Lagerfeld, and Christian Lacroix.

monster hoops

Most likely inspired by farthingales and panniers, the cage crinoline was officially patented in the United States, France, and Britain by an American, W. S. Thomson, in 1856. Despite reaching a diameter of—count 'em—*eighteen feet*, the cage crinoline, at fifty cents to two bucks a pop, was an instant hit. The steel birdcage-shaped contraption needed only one petticoat layered between itself and the topskirt to mask the slats, leaving a breezy little chamber for ladies to kick their legs about or, perhaps, shoplift a ham. Ditching heavy petticoats was a godsend, but long, fancy drawers became essential, as it was discovered that a good wind could catch the large skirt and cause an unwanted peep show.

Like the farthingales before them, the cage crinoline morphed in size and shape. At one point, the metal slats bulged out in the back as though the wearer had just hatched an armadillo. The frame's sloping backside was enhanced with topskirts sprouting layers upon layers of ruffled panels, creating a sort of peacock plumage.

The cage crinoline was clumsy to wear, but ladies could give a flea. It provided the desired, and painful, Cinderella-style hourglass shape, it was cooling and had a kicky kind of swing to it, and if the occasional figurine or serving tea tray was sacrificed to the dustpan gods, so be it. Using a

cage crinoline

chamber pot was a hassle, so ladies drank less tea. Some crinolines were so big that occasionally hostesses couldn't leave their own powder rooms unaided. Candles were cast out and fire grates were avoided at all costs. (In one documented case from 1893, 2,500 Chileans died in a church fire when a devotee's crinoline brushed too close to a prayer candle.) And yet during their heyday, enough steel was produced to make as many as a half-million cage crinolines a week, making it the first mass-produced *couture* item and the first fashion craze.

Pottery workers and china-shop salesgirls were especially at risk but wore them still, even when lawmakers stepped in with attempts to legislate the size of the things. Supernurse Florence Nightingale lashed out against the cage crinoline. In *Notes on Nursing*, she wrote: "Fortunate it is if their skirts do not catch fire and if the nurse does not give herself up a sacrifice together with her patient to be burnt in her own petticoats. I wish the Registrar General would tell us the exact number of deaths by burning occasioned by this absurd and hideous custom."

By 1870, however, even diehard fashionistas heeded the words of humorist Josh Billings: "Fashion makes fools of some, sinners of others, and slaves of all." They ditched the lethal cage crinoline and returned to the tried-and-true multi-layered skirt.

SKIRTING THE LAW:
NINETEENTH-CENTURY EFFORTS
TO LEGISLATE SKIRTS

- In Prussia in 1830, the government enacted a law that cigars must be smoked in a wire-mesh contraption designed to prevent sparks from setting fire to ladies' crinolines and hoopskirts.

- On Sundays, in Elizabeth, New Jersey, it was forbidden for a woman to walk down Broad Street without wearing her petticoats.

- In Charlotte, North Carolina, women had to have their bodies covered by at least sixteen yards of cloth at all times.

- In Europe, common folk could not wear silk guards—decorative embellishments of colorful silk—on their petticoats because silk and other frivolous notions were scarce.

- No person in Grand Haven, Michigan, could throw an abandoned hoopskirt into any street or on any sidewalk, under penalty of a five-dollar fine for each offense.

- In Michigan, it was against the law for a lady to lift her skirt more than six inches while walking through a mud puddle.

- A bill went to the state legislature in 1893 to prohibit the wearing of hoopskirts in Minnesota, sparking greater fury than a pending anti–cigarette smoking bill.

"She extends her authority
to the minutest details of
our lives; tells us when we must
eat and when we must strive
to amuse ourselves. She turns
day into night, ignores
our comforts, disposes of our
money and our time, and
engages in successful war even
with Nature itself."

◇◇◇

**THE RATIONAL
DRESS SOCIETY'S GAZETTE**
on the role of fashion, 1888

CHAPTER 5

BABY GOT BACK

bustles and padded skirts

By the mid-nineteenth century, a dangerous breed of ladies—pesky suffragettes and early feminists—were making waves across America's heartland. Helpless and melancholy was no longer in vogue; today's woman demanded such unspeakable allowances as the right to vote, to speak before spoken to, to seek exercise, and to wear a skirt that could fit through the damn front door. Dressmakers were happy to oblige, and with the cage crinoline on the outs, they came up with new designs that narrowed the skirt but, in keeping with the elaborate style of the era, gathered yards and yards of material back to meet the bum. Enter (or exit, as it would be): the bustle.

Variations of bum padding—the bum roll in particular—had been in use since the fourteenth century, though usually worn under a petticoat or hoopskirt. But in 1864, fashion designer Charles Frederick Worth drove women into a tizzy when he designed a crinoline-free skirt that featured a short train and a horsehair pouf sewn in place above the *derrière*. His new design was shocking because without any boned structure underneath the topskirt, the form of a woman's legs was visible through the fabric as she walked. Thus, legs, for the first time, became a tool of seduction. (We're not talking ZZ Top–style leg action here, but it was a titillating revelation nonetheless.) This style was known as *bouffant tournure*—the term "bustle" was initially considered vulgar among the upper crust.

Crinoline-free skirts became the accepted style. As with farthingales, excess skirt fabric was lifted, draped, and puffed around the skirt like the *polonaise* of the eighteenth century, creating elegant confectionary folds trimmed in fringe, ruffles, and pleats. This was a fantastic era for skirt design, as attention was drawn away from the bodice, and all the artistry was featured on the lower and back parts of the body. Full-length dresses finally moved out of vogue, and the quintessential skirt, paired with a bodice and jacket, was *du jour*.

In the early 1870s, the favored bustle was a boil of a thing, constructed of pads, springs, ruffles, wires, or curved boning and tied around the hips. It sat just above the rump like a cat sleeping on a windowsill. That style soon morphed

skirt with
bustle

into an elongated waterfall, or fishtail, bustle. Far different
from the cat-size bustle, the waterfall was the size—and
weight—of a small child. It reached the back of the knees, was
often adjustable, and had flat side panels that tied in the front.
In favor of the new look, *Harper's Bazaar* wrote in 1876 that
all other "*bouffant tournures* are abandoned" and praised the
new bustle's ability to deflect the fabric from the feet.

Between 1875 and 1883, skirts—featuring the waterfall
bustle and complex tape arrangements that held the drapes,
pleats, and rustles in place—created an increasingly slender

waterfall
bustle

silhouette, especially in the front and sides. Women's bottoms were *the* fetishized body part, but sometimes you can have too much of a good thing ...

take a seat—oh, i see you've brought your own

By the early 1880s, slim was out as quickly as it came in. The cat-on-the-rump-style bustle returned with a vengeance, only now it was the size of a Thanksgiving turkey. Women's behinds protruded almost perpendicular to their waistlines, giving them the profile of a snail. Bustles grew so large that ladies who were used to sitting around on their bums all day couldn't even manage to do that. Some women purportedly shrugged and pushed the thing off to one side, but what if you couldn't gracefully work it back into place upon rising? How would you explain *that* to Lord and Lady Marlborough?

In 1887, actress Lillie Langtry landed the first celebrity lingerie endorsement and lent her name to a bustle that neatly folded up, accordion style, when the wearer sat down.

Because bustle skirts were so narrow, movement was limited to about a six-inch stride. Women, who were at first pleased to learn the crinoline-free designs allowed them to move freely through such previously tight spaces as, say, city sidewalks, quickly realized this freedom didn't mean boo if they couldn't *walk* in the things: The bustled skirts were too damn tight.

With more women in Europe and the U.S. entering the workforce and, for the first time, getting exercise (especially on bicycles), in 1889, the voluminous bustle disappeared practically overnight. The Victorian Look—a prim, high-collared blouse called a shirtwaist, paired with an ankle-length gored skirt, a design stitched in relaxed, tapering pieces that fit smoothly over the hips or with simple back pleats or flares toward the hem—was in vogue. It was hands-down the least restrictive form of the skirt seen since the 1830s— there was no stopping a woman in this liberating number. Sans petticoats, crinolines, and bustle, this Victorian skirt was well suited to walking and other active pursuits. Emphasis was back on the bodice, and skirts became plain Janes, with zero adornment or decoration and simply paired with a rustling silk slip, for a look that was quickly coined "froufrou."

The feminists and their supporters championed the "New Woman," the new generation of energetic and active young women. The term was ridiculed by conservatives and many members of the press, but these nineteenth-century riot grrls forged ahead, seeking freedom and modernity, playing golf and tennis, riding bicycles, pushing suffrage, enrolling in universities, and getting jobs, all while keeping their place in society. Women like this couldn't be tied down with fully boned bustles and interlined outfits, and the dress suit became the uniform of the turn-of-the-twentieth-century New Woman.

FREE YOUR MIND AND THE REST
WILL FOLLOW: RATIONAL DRESS REFORM

Nineteenth-century feminists rallied to break down the restrictive and harmful-to-health fashions—choking corsets, cinched bustles, and binding skirts—that had prohibited women from participating as ordinary members of society for centuries, as well as likely accounting for fainting spells, broken ribs, and other maladies. The first dress reformers were the female political idealists of the French Revolution, who championed women in trousers, a sentiment echoed by a smattering of pioneering women—and a few men—in the United States, especially in rural and western territories where the hard work of settling new land justified such a practicality. It took nearly 100 years, though, for the Rational Dress Society (RDS) to organize in 1881 in London and publicly raise awareness to the dangers of restrictive corsetry and other fashion immobilities. The RDS promoted the belief that women should not have to wear more than *seven* pounds of undergarments at a time, as opposed to the average fourteen, and considered fashion an exploitation of the workers—namely seamstresses—who produced it. The RDS's *Gazette* published six issues between 1888 and 1889 and saw significant coverage from feminist journals such as *Women's Penny Paper* and *Woman's Signal*, though most women's magazines wouldn't have any of it and newspaper coverage was more mystified than scornful. The popularity of bicycling as a sport for both sexes fast-forwarded the acceptance of women in casual, looser and lighter clothing, such as divided skirts, a kind of old-fashioned gaucho. From then on, women were thrilled by the freedom of having fashion options beyond heavy skirts, albeit not always unrestrictive ones.

"If women want to run for governor, they ought to be able to run for a car.... If they want to be legally free they shouldn't be sartorially shackled.... There are some so unkind to suggest that trousers would have been better—far better—and much more comfortable [than the hobble skirt]."

◇◇◇

THE NEW YORK TIMES,
June 12, 1910

CHAPTER 6

FETTERED CALVES

the hobble skirt

A t the dawn of the twentieth century, ladies were getting increasingly vocal about their demands for equality, and yet the Gibson Girl—popular illustrator Charles Dana Gibson's Edwardian nameless Barbie-esque icon, an agreeable and serene fashion plate—became the ideal. Since her introduction in the 1890s, her pretty image with long, piled hair, swooping plumed hat, a neat shirtwaist, and a gored skirt was mass-merchandised over the next two decades with the kind of fervor that would come to define twentieth-century American capitalism: illustrations, dolls, wallpaper, linens, songs, plays, books—you name it. Despite— or even because of—cries for equal opportunity, a subordi- nate paradigm of a woman was still desired. Skirt hems started to shrink inward, and became more binding than ever before.

The simply cut gored skirt of the late 1800s began the new century clingy and S-shaped, giving it a mermaid effect. Some featured trains with overly decorated hems of ruffles and lace. Then waistlines began to rise after 1905, eventually returning to the high, under-the-bosom Empire length by 1910, in what was called the Empire Revival style. Crisp silk taffetas and stiff wools gave way to soft, fluid silks and initially, the raised waistline was combined with a very full bottom hem, allowing much freedom of movement. Then, in the spring of 1910, the roomy skirt was abruptly narrowed at the knee, creating a shackling effect that literally hobbled the women wearing them.

don't get up. no, really.

The hobble skirt, invented by French couturier Paul Poiret in 1910, all but eliminated stepping and striding. The legend goes that Poiret was inspired by the plucky ingenuity of one Mrs. Hart O. Berg, the first woman to ride in an airplane. Prior to takeoff, Mrs. Berg had tied a rope around her legs to keep her skirt from flapping midair. Poiret, either inspired or titillated, copied the woman's awkward decent from the plane and slapped a fat price tag on it. Fashion victims loved it.

The more accurate story behind Poiret's inspiration, however, is that the hobble likely evolved as a kinkier descendant of the kimono-style dress he had introduced in his Oriental-inspired collection the year before. Despite the S&M

hobble
skirt

"THE METHOD IN THE MADNESS"

Her hobble skirts so very tight
She cannot dance at all by night.
And when she goes to walk with me
Along the moonlit Summer sea.
What wonder that my pulses stir
To think that I must carry her!

CARLYLE SMITH,
Rhymester's Notes, September 11, 1910

nature of the hobble, Poiret's designs were considered refreshing. He ushered in the twentieth-century woman, banished corsets, and, in his words, "freed the bosom, shackled the legs, but gave liberty to the body."

Bound tightly at the shins and waist but full at the thighs, the hobble gave ladies, whether sitting awkwardly or cruelly struggling along the street, the appearance of a fettered calf. Newspapers had a field day with women's wiggling, insect-like pace, running satirical cartoons and commentary about the absurdity and danger of wearing a garment one couldn't walk in, particularly in an age of speeding automobiles and progressive politics. "The Hobble is the Latest Freak in Women's Fashions," *The New York Times* declared incredulously in June of 1910, joking that women would need to depend on their hopscotch skills to get around. "The amazing part of it," the writer continued, "is that the women don't seem to care whether they can walk or not as long as they can have one of those skirts." On its own, however, the skirt apparently wasn't an adequate enough impediment for fashion victims. These poor gals, unused to taking such mincing steps, kept tearing seams and splitting their skirts, so in came the hobble garter, a bestial undergarment strapped firmly around the shins that limited stride length further and rendered the wearer even more subordinate. But their seams, at least, were safe.

Throughout the summer of 1910, hobble-related injuries were reported on a weekly basis. Women tripped on stairs boarding streetcars, avoiding fast-moving vehicles, and catching their heels on the hems. Tragedy was inevitable, of course, and in Paris that September, a hobbled woman was unable to dodge a running horse and was trampled to death. Several more deaths followed over the years, yet hobble naysayers were primarily confined to suffragette rallies and editorial pages during the throes of the skirt's popularity. Even the *New York Times*, which went from disgusted to bemused, kicked off 1912 with a two-column instructional article on "Walking in Hobble Skirts," insisting that if the hobble were truly here to stay, then young women must learn a more sedate and dignified manner of walking in them.

The hobble combo kept ladies grounded—literally. A neat new invention called the automobile was all the rage,

SPORTSWEAR

"I think bicycling," said Susan B. Anthony in 1896, "has done more to emancipate women than anything else in the world." Despite being shackled in hobbles, the Edwardian lady was fairly active, thanks initially to bicycling, which, when introduced twenty years prior, gave women their first taste of independence—and more variety in their wardrobes. While still in skirts, these plucky gals also tackled tennis, croquet, swimming, golf, fencing, riding, and now, motoring, and with these new pursuits came style necessities. Cycling was the first sport to develop its own style of clothing in the 1890s, with special bicycle dresses worn with leggings or bloomers, and underskirts were outfitted with interior straps for keeping the fabric from blowing in the wind. For other sports, hems were raised and skirts were roomier, though still smart and tailored. By 1910, golf dresses had pleats down the sides to prevent tearing, and in 1917, *Vogue* encouraged women to stow their topskirts in knapsacks and take to ski slopes in their jodhpurs. Alice Marble strode onto the tennis court at Wimbledon in white shorts in 1932, and a few years later trousers were considered acceptable for all sports.

bicycle skirt

and hobbled women found they could no longer climb up on its running boards. In 1912, New York City trolley cars were refitted with lower boarding steps, and railway stations provided special stairs to make it easier for ladies to board the trains. But while the hobble won some battles, it lost others: In 1911, schoolgirls were banned from wearing hobbles during graduation ceremonies in Washington, D.C., and that same year Queen Mary barred the hobble from High Court, noting a woman couldn't possibly curtsy in one. In the end, the Model T was a greater temptress than fashion: Ladies were itching to get behind the wheel, and many abandoned the hobble for more leg room. The hobble skirt fell out of favor after about five years, but the lore it left behind is timeless.

Poiret said his success was due to giving women exactly what they always craved—freedom—and in some ways, that's what they got. The popularity of the hobble, though short-lived, proves that women were calling the shots and relishing the independence of it, comfort be damned. Ever the slave to fashion, a clotheshorse still had a breadth of choices in her wardrobe, and if handicapped was what she wanted, well, that's what she would get. Interestingly, hobbles were brought back into popularity in the 1950s as a bondage and fetish item and enjoy a large and loyal following today. Thus, you might not want to Google "hobble skirt" while at the office.

"I don't see how
an article of clothing
can be indecent.
A person, yes."

◇◇◇

ROBERT A. HEINLEIN,
controversial science fiction author

CHAPTER 7

REBELS WITH A CAUSE

flappers

Blame it on the stress of Prohibition or the spoils of a strong economy, but after World War I you couldn't keep those votin', smokin', dancin' broads down. A new era of decidedly scandalous women called flappers were driving cars, bobbing their hair, shimmying in their skirts—cut shorter for better access to the bootleg whiskey flask stowed in a garter belt—and for the first time exposing (gasp!) shins. The skirt itself was a shapeless sack, but a well-placed Charleston kick bared a little bit of knee.

The word *flapper* was coined sometime in the teens to describe rebellious girls who dressed casually and flaunted "modern" attitudes. The bob haircut was introduced in New York by celebrity dancer Irene Castle in 1914; she'd seen fashionable Parisians wearing it, knocked it off, and made the

"MARY'S LITTLE SKIRT"

Mary had a little skirt,
The latest style no doubt.
But every time she got inside
She was more than halfway out.

JOHN ROACH STRATTON,
The *New York Times*,
June 27, 1921

style a sensation. But the quintessential "flapper look" as we know it today didn't develop until about 1921. Far more than just a short skirt and bobbed haircut, to properly pull off the style one needed a whole lot of hepcat attitude. Standing with shoulders slouched over, cigarette raised, pelvis jutted forward, and (ideally) scrawny hipbones protruding from a corset-free filmy skirt, the flapper was all about posturing. The typical wardrobe was unfitted and baggy: Coats were belted loosely at the waist but left rakishly open, and galoshes—the heavy-soled, all-weather walking shoe of choice—were always left unbuckled. These wide-open, flapping galoshes are one theory on how the word *flapper* originated; another is that these young women were like fledglings, flapping their wings and struggling to leave the nest. Flappers cursed like sailors, wore garish makeup, held petting parties, and coined their own mysterious, jazzy slang—"cat's pajamas," "bee's knees," and "big cheese" are just a few of the many holdover sayings from that era.

flapper skirt

floating panels

Grown-ups and a growing conservative religious segment couldn't stand the ballsy gals. Looking back, flappers were the quintessential hip-hoppers of their generation.

In 1920, skirt lengths were long and reached almost to the ankle, but by 1921 they were six inches from the floor. By 1925, they had moved up to eight inches; by 1926 and 1927, they were fourteen, sixteen—even eighteen—inches from the ground. It was still unusual to see a dress cut above the knee, but with all the mad dancing, street strutting, and chaise-sprawling, a kneecap was sure to peep forth. These gals knew what they were doing: They even heavily rouged or powdered their knees to ensure the extra skin wouldn't escape attention.

Throughout the 1920s, one-piece styles—a straight hanging dress with a drop waist and no curves—dominated. Some dresses featured big belts that weren't cinched but merely slung around the hip line. For the first time, the ideal silhouette was that of a child, with flat chest and no hips (*Vogue* magazine warned, "If you have [a flat abdomen] not—go get it"), and new lingerie, "the bra," was introduced to keep boobs in place during especially rollicking rounds of Charleston shimmies.

With the Art Deco movement on the rise, artistic, uneven hemlines came into vogue toward the late end of the decade, and skirts became far more complex. Long, floating panels of fabric dropped from the waistline and over the skirt. Flares, pleats, and gathers were placed off-center, scallops or pointed jester-like segments ran along the edge of hemlines, and draped and layered fabrics achieved handker-chief-skirt styles. Intricate decorative beading and geometric-patterned fabrics were favored, and chiffon, soft satins, velvets, and silk taffeta replaced wool and cotton as frequently used fabrics. As for the all-over fringe number we associate with flappers today, despite what modern-day Halloween costume makers want you to believe, it wasn't a prevalent look.

To accompany the free-spirited, newfangled style, girls needed a fresh healthy look. Until World War I, women had covered up their bodies from the sun, associating suntans with lower-class folks and unseemly day laborers. In France, though, "It" designer Gabrielle "Coco" Chanel adored soaking up the rays, and so sure she was of the sun's healing powers that she convinced the entire world of it. Chanel crowed, "A girl should be two things: classy and fabulous," and to be so she needed an allover bronze glow. Borrowing the sweater and jersey fabrics issued to infantrymen, Chanel created loose, shoulder-and-leg-baring resort wear meant to be accessorized with tanned skin. Single-handedly and nearly overnight, Chanel brought the suntan into fashion. Without her vision of a bronzed world, the careers of bathing beauties Betty Grable, Sally "Gidget" Fields, Brigitte Bardot, and a slew of Bond Girls—not to mention that of thousands of dermatologists and wrinkle-cream manufacturers—might have been hopelessly hindered.

There was one other skirt style available during the flapper era, a popular substitute for the hard-to-achieve slim silhouette. In 1919, designer Jeanne Lanvin introduced the *robe de style*, a bouffant skirt with a dropped waistline, where the seam is positioned at the hips rather than the waist, and a full, poufy skirt. Though this style was flattering on robust girls, most women opted for the favored—and more svelte—look of the era.

robe de style

To say the flapper era was a fashion and social revolution is an understatement. As Chanel noted at the time, "Youth is something very new. Twenty years ago no one mentioned it." Before the First World War, the demure and thoughtful nature of the post-Victorian Gibson Girl was the favored personality. By contrast, Flappers drank bootleg whiskey and bathtub gin straight up, and danced all night to the Black Bottom—ladies and gents spanking their backsides with one hand, thrusting back and forth, stamping feet, and gyrating hips.

For the first time, youth was at the forefront, defining what would later be coined pop culture, and conservative society was in an uproar. In 1921, the Y.W.C.A. was distributing anti-flapper tracts on the proper and improper way to dress. ("Proper dress" would mirror the costumes of the old cronies, who still wore modest Victorian-style ankle-length skirts.) Throughout that year, educational institutions barred flappers from attending classes, and no church, ladies' club, or lecture hall was exempt from a heated discussion about reforming America's out-of-control young women. Restrictions and bans on the flappers' clothing and behavior continued unabated through the decade. In Salem, Indiana, in 1927, the town marshal ordered a ban on unfastened galoshes, declaring the open footwear a nuisance. In Rome that same year, the women's fascist organization was one of many social groups across Europe that precluded "flappers and tomboys" from membership—as if the girls cared.

The flappers incited an early (albeit short-lived) debate on economic politics. Conservative male journalists spewed venom at flappers, pointing out that by wearing short skirts these girls were dismantling great American institutions like baggage transfer companies, which declared bankruptcy across the country: "Ladies who used to go away for the summer with six trunks can now pack twenty dainty costumes in a bag," cried the New Republic in 1925. Fabric manufacturers wailed as their orders plummeted (smaller skirts, after all, mean less fabric), and certain areas of manufacturing, such as skirt bindings, became obsolete.

For their part, many women chimed in saying that men should butt out of the discussion and that women should decide what women should wear. In 1925, journalist Bruce Blevin prophesized optimistically that "Feminism has won a victory. . . . Women have highly resolved that they are just as good as men, and intend to be treated so. . . . They clearly mean (even though not all of them yet realize it) that in the great game of sexual religion they shall no longer be forced to play the role, simulated or real, of helpless quarry."

The flapper look was over by the end of 1927, with fashion reports in the New York Times gushing about the longer, draped hemlines of the upcoming season, calling the new skirts "the plump woman's kindest friend."

FLAPPER SLANG

Like the Eskimos with their many words for snow, the flappers had numerous ways to say "drunk." Slinking around speakeasies and frequently on the lam from the cops, the dames of the 1920s created a lingo all their own.

ALL WET: Describes a dumb idea or individual, as in, "He's all wet."

AND HOW: I strongly agree!

BALONEY: Nonsense!

BEAT IT: Scram or get lost

BEE'S KNEES: An amazing person, thing, idea; the ultimate

BEEF: A complaint or to complain

BEESWAX: Business, as in, "None of your beeswax."

BIG CHEESE: The most important or influential person; boss. (Same as big shot.)

BLIND DATE: Going out with someone you've never met

BULL SESSION: Male gossip, stories of sexual exploits

BUM'S RUSH: Ejection by force from an establishment

CANNED: Drunk. Also: corked, embalmed, fried to the hat, jazzed, lit, ossified, owled, plastered, primed, scrooched, spifflicated, tanked, zozzled

CAPER: A criminal act or robbery

CARRY A TORCH: To have a crush on someone

CAT'S MEOW or **CAT'S PAJAMAS**: Something splendid or stylish; similar to bee's knees

CRUSH: An infatuation

DAME: A female

DAPPER: A flapper's dad

DOGS: Feet

DOLL: An attractive woman

DOLLED UP: Dressed up

DOUBLE-CROSS: To cheat, stab in the back

DRUGSTORE COWBOY: A guy that hangs around on street corners trying to pick up girls

DUMB DORA: A stupid female

FALL GUY: Victim of a setup

FIRE EXTINGUISHER: A chaperone

FLY BOY: A dreamy term for an aviator

GAMS: A woman's legs

GET A WIGGLE ON: Get a move on, get going

GOLD DIGGER: A woman who goes after a man for his money

HAIR OF THE DOG: Liquor

HANDCUFF: Engagement ring

HARD-BOILED: Tough

HIGH-HAT: To snub

HOOCH: Bootleg liquor

HOOFER: Dancer

IT: Sex appeal

JANE: Any female

JALOPY: Old car

JAVA AND JOE: Coffee

JOHN: A toilet

JOINT: An establishment

JUICE JOINT: A speakeasy

KEEN: Attractive or appealing

KISSER: Mouth

LEVEL WITH ME: Be honest

LINE: Insincere flattery

LIVE WIRE: A lively person

NECK: Kissing with passion

NIFTY: Great, excellent

ON THE LAM: Fleeing from police

ON THE LEVEL: Legitimate, honest

PET: Same as neck, but more so

PINCH: To arrest

PIPE DOWN: Stop talking

PUTTING ON THE RITZ: Doing something in high style; named for the Hôtel Ritz in Paris.

RAZZ: To make fun of

REAL McCOY: Authentic

SAP: A fool

SAYS YOU: A reaction of disbelief

SCRAM: Leave immediately

SHIV: A knife

SPEAKEASY: An illegal establishment selling bootleg liquor

SPIFFY: An elegant appearance

STRUGGLE BUGGY: The backseat of a car. A parent's worst nightmare.

SWELL: Wonderful. Also: a rich man

TOMATO: A female

WET BLANKET: A killjoy

WHAT'S EATING YOU?: What's wrong?

WHOOPEE: To have a good time

YOU SLAY ME: You're funny.

"Darling, the legs
aren't so beautiful, I just know
what to do with them."

◇◇◇

MARLENE DIETRICH,
screen siren

CHAPTER 8

CRASHING DOWN

the stock-market skirt

Just as the ladies got their long-overdue fashion liberation, the stock market crashed, and with it, hemlines. And with poverty comes conservatism: Skirts became dowdy and functional, more narrow and prudish with zero sex appeal. It was bad enough being poor, but now women can't get any action either? Oh, the humanity!

In the Roaring Twenties, America had experienced a decade of delish excess, but Black Monday 1929 launched a ten-plus-year-long depression. As money became scarcer and consumers practiced more puritanical values, there was less partying, less fun, and a whole lot less leg. Almost immediately, hemlines began creeping down the shin. In the years following the crash, skirt lengths landed ten to twelve inches above the ground, and some styles came as low as the ankle.

drab and drabber

The silver screen was one of the few industries that boomed during the Great Depression. Movie stars wore ultra-glamorous, leave-nothing-to-the-imagination fashions and lived in a fantasy world of divine decadence that did not reflect the reality of the American experience. The conservative movement, still preening its ruffled feathers over the flapper era and waylaid by the 1933 repeal of Prohibition, sounded the alarm at the nudity and raunch of early films. In 1934, the government established the Hays Code, a strict docket of regulations that required movie studios to restrict what its writers considered degenerate behavior, outlawing suggestive clothing, language, scenarios, and gestures. The Code forbid sexy clothing, because "transparent or translucent materials and silhouette are frequently more suggestive than actual exposure." This backlash against freedom of expression was a direct result of the anything-goes behavior of the Roaring Twenties, and as the Code put it, "wrong entertainment lowers the whole living conditions and moral ideals of a race." The Hays Code didn't only impact the silver screen. On the streets, filmgoers took a cue from their favorite stars and dropped hem too.

Through the 1930s, fickle skirt lengths rose and fell with the mental state of the country. Hemlines generally held below the knee, necklines rose, and the overall cut of women's clothing became much boxier and more modest. By the middle of the decade, the optimism generated by the New Deal—Roosevelt's plan to save the economy— brightened spirits, and skirts crept slightly upward, reaching thirteen and fourteen inches off the ground. But as soon as the Second World War broke out in Europe and Paris was quickly occupied, fashion plummeted to new depths of dowdy. Wartime utility clothing, the lowest low in fashionable fashion history (after the medieval dirndl) became the standard costume for Westerners through the war years. For the time being, the multifaceted days of the skirt were over.

Restraint and practicality were the main features of clothing during the war; "Make do and mend" was the reigning motto of the time. In June 1941, rationing restricted the amount of cloth allowed in garment manufacturing. The amount of fabric, number of buttons, pleats, and pockets for each garment was controlled, and unnecessary padding or decoration was outlawed. Clothes were made with the minimum of material, tinier hems, and narrower seams and were labeled CC41, as in Clothing Control 1941. Women were given coupons to buy skirts and other clothes, and an illegal black market for these coupons fostered under the demand. Not that the skirts available were worth getting arrested for. Nylon, silk, and wool were scarce.

wartime utility skirt

The general silhouette was quite plain and square; skirts were straight and fit poorly, and reflected military styles. All detailing was eliminated, leaving garments slipshod. Only wedding dresses and burial gowns were exempt from restrictions.

By the early 1940s, the hem had risen to a promising sixteen inches from the ground, but most skirts were still quite plain—without many patterns and even fewer embellishments—and no amount of leg could make them especially alluring. Pleats were becoming popular, though, and many skirts featured a short kick pleat in the back, or one or two narrow pleats in the front. Around 1944, frills and peplums, ruffle-like fabric attached to the edge of clothing, were used in skirts to give a sort of bustle effect at the back. Shirring—which gathered material into rows using decorative stitching—was used at the waistline to give a somewhat fuller effect, but the basic look, especially in Europe, was very boxy and military-influenced. It was a definite low point for the skirt.

With the war over and the economy booming, the end of the 1940s saw a return to elegance, and hemlines rose to seventeen inches off the ground. Coupons and clothing restrictions disappeared altogether in 1949, and seamstresses were able to embellish and tailor to their hearts' content.

kick pleat skirt

Since the Depression and the subsequent finicky nature of hemlines through World War II, the height of hemlines has been used as a barometer to determine the outlook of the stock market. Though market analysts didn't pick up on the connection at the time, the Skirt Length Theory, an indicator of market value and consumer behavior, was born. The thinking behind the theory goes that shorter skirts tend to appear in times when general consumer confidence is high, and when hemlines fall and skirts are worn longer, the overall outlook is gloomy and fearful. (The same goes for lipstick sales, according to Leonard Lauder, the chairman of Estée Lauder.) In 1971, hot pants were the rage, and the advice at the Dow Jones was, "Don't sell until you see the heights of their thighs!" Now in the twenty-first century, with hemlines all over the place, the Skirt Length Theory serves only as a cute colloquialism of the past.

"Not so fast, my skirt's
too tight!"

"I told you you didn't
know how to
dress for a murder."

◇◇◇

**CAROLE LANDIS AND
GEORGE MURPHY**
in *Having a Wonderful Crime*, 1945

CHAPTER 9

COLD-WAR YEARS

the pencil skirt

The pencil skirt is one of those strange throwback pieces that has enjoyed nearly unwavering popularity since its introduction in the late 1940s. High-waisted and skintight down to its abrupt mid-calf hemline, the original pencil had fashion victim written all over it. Despite magazines quipping such advice as "You can be just as chic in this long, crippling hobble," women, frustrated by the brisk military-style fashions of the time, tripped over themselves to time-travel back three fashion decades and squeeze into the tight sausage casings. Never mind the fact that one had to take baby steps when wearing the thing; women simply adopted the wiggle-walk, reminiscent of a waif stricken with polio, that had been perfected during the short reign of the hobble skirt thirty years earlier.

Luggage brown and gray-toned, calf-length, hobble-style skirts in wool and silk were (re)introduced in 1947 by French designer Jacques Fath and quickly dubbed pencil skirts. Of Fath's "brilliant opening" that winter, the *New York Times* reviewed the new silhouette: "draped and spiraling...skirts twist about the figure so tightly and are so long, about fourteen inches from the floor, that only mincing steps are possible." London's *Picture Post* was more direct: "The mannequins can hardly walk." The 35-year-old brute skyrocketed to fame, becoming one of the most sought-after designers after Christian Dior. Of his position Fath remarked, "Fashion is an art and men are the artists." Um, right. That is, if by "fashion" he means shackling garments designed to cripple, then, yes, he is a freaking artist.

Poor fashion models really did suffer. Often posed with one leg angled awkwardly forward and the skirt pinned impossibly tight in the back to underscore its willowy proper-ties, twig-thin "mannequins" were expected to perform a serious of perverse twists and turns—without falling over, not to mention breaking a kneecap.

Of course, one bondage item spawns another. Our old friend the corset—now in an elongated, tighter package—was unearthed from the mothballs, dusted off, and secured back around hips and bellies.

Naturally, the highest of heels were the just-right shoe to elongate the figure and were accompanied with a smart,

pencil skirt

tailored suit jacket and bodice, as if the pencil was part of a business skirt. Turned ankles, forfeited taxis, and missed meetings were a small price for such smart, clean lines.

Thankfully, in 1947, the circle skirt and all its petticoats came along to help women kick up their heels again, though through the 1950s the pencil remained an alternative to the new flouncy skirts.

The sixties and seventies were nearly pencil-free zones, but by the early 1980s the old tight skirt was back. This time, though, new stretchy fabrics and shorter lengths (at the knee and higher) moved the pencil past "hobble" into just plain sexy—if not occasionally tacky; it *was* the eighties after all.

CLOSE SHAVE

Not surprisingly, the advent of leg shaving coincided with the rise of skirt hemlines. Women were first addressed as potential shavers in the May 1915 issue of *Harper's Bazaar*. In an ad displaying a young woman, arms raised, and her pits bare, the text trumpeted: "Summer Dress and Modern Dancing combine to make necessary the removal of objectionable hair." By 1922, the Sears catalog did brisk business in women's razors and hair-removal products. Leg hair, though, took a while longer to conquer because gals had stockings or skirts to cover up. Come World War II and pinup girl Betty Grable's fantastic—and clean-shaven—gams, and baboon legs became as taboo as tattoos. With the war raging, silk stockings were scarce, so smart women made quick use of the razors their G.I. hubbies, dads, and brothers left behind and drew lines with a marker up the back of their newly smooth legs to create a mock stocking look.

Of course, now hair removal of all sorts is a *de rigueur* cosmetic ritual for women. Men, with the exception of speed-seeking athletes, haven't quite caught on—yet.

SEE JANE'S SKIRT GROW

The evolution of the skirt from the early 1930s through the late 1940s can be observed in no better Petri dish than the Hollywood movie serial of Tarzan films, starring Johnny Weissmuller as Tarzan and Maureen O'Sullivan as Jane. A rapid transformation in fashion occurred over the course of this era due to the strict censorship regulations of the Hays Code. The first two films, *Tarzan, the Ape Man* and *Tarzan and His Mate* (both made in the early 1930s), had Jane wearing a bikini top and micro-mini that would make twenty-first-century celebutantes blush, and the jungle lovers have a full-frontal coed swimming scene that would easily earn an R-rating today. In *Tarzan Escapes*, released in 1936, Jane swapped her two-piece for a modest dress that ended a few inches above her knee. In 1939, the couple were so stripped of their lust that in *Tarzan Finds a Son* the audience is spared the sordid details of conception and a child literally falls from the sky. A few years

later, Jane played the fishwife while barefoot and cooking in the tree-house kitchen in *Tarzan's Secret Treasure* (1941), clad in a depressing below-the-knee, unshapely wartime utilitarian skirt. All the while Jane's skirt grew longer, Tarzan's loincloth remained micro, underscoring the differences in the studio's frigid rules regarding what was acceptable for men and for women. By the time the couple hit Manhattan to search for their kidnapped son in *Tarzan's New York Adventure* (1942), Jane and Tarzan were covered head to toe in chic Big City fashions, and one never would have guessed these two had ever shown any skin.

Tarzan's New York Adventure was the last charismatic pairing of Weissmuller and O'Sullivan. The ape man films were still churned out with other actors at a near-annual production rate into the 1950s and early 1960s, though Jane's skirt would never reach the thigh-baring lengths of the original two films. After forty years, the industry finally banished the Hays Code in 1967 and brought sex—and sexy dressing—back to Hollywood, just in time for a new slough of Tarzan adventures.

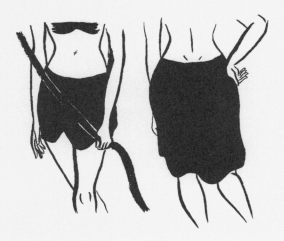

"Ignorant people in preppy clothes
are more dangerous to
America than oil embargoes."

◇◇◇

V. S. NAIPAUL,
Nobel Prize–winning author

CHAPTER 10

THE BIRTH OF PREPPY

coeds in kilts

The Highland kilt has a long history as a military and marrying garment for Scots, but most American women only adopted the pleated tartan look during the collegiate-chic craze of the late 1950s. Thanks to elongated cardigans, jaunty pageboy caps, Peter Pan–collared blouses (all of which can be proudly lettered with the wearer's alma mater insignia), and kilt-like pleated skirts, the inescapable image of the "preppy" was established.

Preppies and their many pleats have their first origins in the college and university boom across the U.S. in the late nineteenth century. Institutions of higher education were launching at a rapid pace, offering middle-class folks the opportunity to excel alongside the muckety-mucks of high society. Diplomas were a new social mark that distinguished the upper-middle from the lower-middle class. As the Wizard of Oz proclaimed in some way or another: Anyone can have a brain, but earning a diploma is what makes a man a great thinker. For a nineteenth-century woman, that diploma was the ticket to landing one of those great thinkers. The university quad became the first place where ladies and gents mixed without the supervision of parents, and an atmosphere for examination of and experimentation with social values, attitudes, and self-expression blossomed. The gals were expected to be on their best behavior and to wear modest and chaste outfits, but they couldn't resist the world-weary, casual elite style the coolest guys favored. By the end of the 1920s, trendy coeds were looking a little boyish, adopting a sporty-smart version of the men's look, swapping out jodhpurs for sassy pleated skirts with zippers—raccoon coat, megaphone, ukulele, and hip flask included.

Traditional Scottish kilts require a skilled tailor and nine yards of fabric (hence the phrase, "the whole nine yards"), but an American college coed in 1931 could make do with a cute wool number from Woolworth's for $16.95. As the ad claims, this mass-made, kilt-like zippered skirt, "in gay bold checks and plaids characteristic of spring," gave them "the casual boyish grace that is the soul of the new fashion."

During the 1930s, college-bound preps wore knee-length pleated or gored skirts in plain nonpatterned fabrics along with simple blouses with letterman-type cardigans. By the late

pleated skirt

collegiate kilts

1940s, pleats were so popular they appeared in skirts, blouses, and jackets, and could be placed at all angles, from horizontal to vertical and even diagonally. During the 1950s, though, East Coast college coeds flaunted more girlish qualities, with just-above-the-knee plaid skirts and pleated kilts of the traditional Highland variety, paired with Peter Pan–collared blouses, tucked-in sweaters, and saddle shoes or penny loafers with long argyle socks cuffed below the knees.

The new kilts were still a far cry from the Highlander original. The structure was basically the same: a wrap skirt folded every inch or so across the back into inch-wide pleats and sometimes fastened with a large safety pin to keep the front aprons closed when walking. American kilt-wearing women needn't go commando like the Scots—some kilts were sold with matchy-matchy woolen panties for windy bike rides and blustery days.

In 1954, *Life* magazine ran a story about the "abbreviated skirt loosely called a kilt" that was the rage on campus, and the *New York Times* mused that coed fashions such as the kilt reflected a state of mind—just what frame of mind was anyone's guess. (Coeds shrugged and said the colorful plaid kilts were a natural progression from the other garish campus craze—loud unisex Bermuda shorts.) The preppy, as we know her today, had become a fashion force that was both widely imitated (think a young Audrey Hepburn) and despised (think *The Catcher in the Rye*'s famously self-loathing Holden Caulfield).

For the first time, clothes were mass-marketed specifically to teens and young girls rather than adult women. Junior and college sections exploded in department stores. Girls would no longer settle for wearing smaller versions of grownups' wardrobes; they were a singular demographic to be reckoned with, flaunting their own unique style, with music, movie stars, and films all their own.

The sporty kilt lives on with Catholic schoolgirls and New England bluebloods, and, of course, men. In the late 1980s, designer Jean Paul Gaultier—who loves to employ humor and irony in his designs—introduced skirts for men: pleated kilts patterned in tartans and globally inspired prints.

Kilt-loving ladies took heart with the skirt's small (as in "micro-mini") revival in the early part of the twenty-first century, alongside the resurgence of Izods, docksiders, and other 1980s ironic Waspy accoutrements. But this time the kilt held its own in a provocative, fetish-fueled fashion zone. For the first time, kilts crept up the thigh with a nod to the chaste schoolgirl fantasy and were worn with a cheeky sluttishness—a far cry from the serious-minded and sensible college coed of the fifties.

"The sounds of petticoats,
its scent, and its ability
to make the lady that much
more inaccessible—
so exciting—makes it a
unique garment."

◇◇◇

ANN FOGERTY,
author of *Wife Dressing: The Fine Art of
Being a Well-Dressed Wife*, 1959

CHAPTER 11

FELT FANCY

the poodle skirt

We all know the poodle skirt as the iconic symbol of the 1950s, a carefree, kicky era of drive-in movies, middle-class barbecues, and young women donning the most amusing throwback to adolescence since rompers and pinafores.

The structural design of the poodle skirt itself was pretty swell. A large full circle of fabric was nipped at the waist with a snug waistband and fitted zipper. The skirt was most popular with saddle-shoed bobby-soxers, and the oversize shape made it perfect for dancing. It swung. It flipped. It helped a twenty-ish Erin Moran play a happy-go-lucky teenager on *Happy Days*.

But add mountains of poufy petticoats underneath and a silly canine appliqué to the front, and any semblance of

dior's new look

allure was thrown to the dogs. As many as eleven yards of fabric were required to accommodate the full-circle skirt pattern. The fabric wasn't light, crisp silk or slippery satin— it was thick felt. Still, all this material made women feel ultra-feminine and extra girlie.

No one knows who first pressed a prancing French poodle onto a circle skirt. Some credit opera singer Juli Lynne Charlot, who had a line of appliquéd circle skirts at Lord & Taylor, but the fad was essentially an ugly step-child descended from Christian Dior's revolutionary "New Look," his debut collection of high-end women's wear introduced to the world in Paris on February 12, 1947. Structured with petticoats, Dior's huge circle skirts, swinging from the waspy waists of diminutive but busty models, caused an uproar. For years women had sacrificed *haute couture* for the war effort. Strict regulations decreed that clothes could not be discarded before they were worn through, and military-style skirts were crafted with no more than three yards of fabric.

In the face of all that, the unknown Dior rebelliously cut as much as twenty-five yards of luxurious, expensive fabric for his skirts. He cinched his models into corsets and heavily

poodle skirt

padded their hips and breasts, bringing back the nineteenth-century hourglass figure. Newswires buzzed with details about the shocking collection, and women around the world were alternately enraptured with and enraged by the designer's audacity.

Postwar fashionistas were attacked on the streets of Paris for wearing the New Look. Stateside, women balked at the thought of discarding their sensible and comfortable wartime wear and signed anti-Dior petitions or joined action groups to oppose his binding corsets and heavily petticoated skirts. The Georgia State Legislature tried to outlaw his clothes. (Apparently, Christian Dior was a greater threat than Jim Crow.) Bessie Braddock, a member of British Parliament, condemned the look as "the ridiculous whim of idle people." But once the people caught a glimpse of Rita Hayworth in Dior's full Soirée gown at the premiere of *Gilda*, idle suddenly looked pretty darn swanky. The New Look was swiftly adopted and readily adapted. "It doesn't matter what they say about you, as long as they say it on the front page," Dior quipped in triumph.

Soon boxy skirts were all but abandoned in favor of the hourglass. Felt, which was inexpensive and had the *oomph* needed to make skirts really drape and swing, became a favored fabric for many home seamstresses. In war-ravaged England, dressmaker Dereta evaded fabric rations and clothing coupons by making 700 New Look–style garments in budget-conscious gray flannel, while ordinary women put their air-raid blackout curtains to use as skirt fabric. Savvy French seamstresses combined two or more skirts to make one, and often patch-worked patriotic colors into their designs in an effort to win over those for whom the war effort was all too fresh. Around the world, gals faithfully washed perky petticoats in sugar water and dried them over umbrellas to keep their shape.

In 1950, *Life* magazine mused, "By all the rules of fashion logic the newly popular circle skirts make no sense," but allowed that they were ideal for home entertaining as they were immediate conversation pieces. The large, novel patterns that blanketed the skirts, which were dubbed "conversation circles," soon morphed into whimsical appliquéd motifs: music notes, lettering, kitty-cats, and, in honor of the world's love affair with the newly liberated Paris, a happy, prancing poodle.

In 1952, New York designer Bettie Murrie hatched Parlor Game Skirts, wide circle skirts appliquéd with felt backgammon and bingo boards. In this demure precursor to Twister, the wearer was encouraged to hunker down on the floor and allow partygoers to gather 'round her hemline for a lively game. Never mind that the sprawling hostess was held hostage on her knees while her guests played,

parlor game skirt

fashion was back! Rosie the Riveter was officially put out to pasture.

By 1955, the cutesy trend was still in full swing but flagging. Mid-century tweenie boutique the Jayne Thorpe Shops placed an ad that barked, "Our Snooty Poodle Skirt is a captivating bit of dogfoolery," suggesting that by this time even its makers got the joke: The circle skirt had gone from Paris *haute couture* to lowbrow snark.

With the exception of devoted square dance enthusiasts, circle skirts have come in and out of fashion over the past five decades, but never with the same postwar enthusiasm or the piles of rustling petticoats that made the skirts such an iconic distinction of the 1950s.

THE POODLE NEVER DIES

No fashion motif has reigned as long as the poodle. The skirt and its most popular icon was a fifties mainstay. During the mid 1970s, punk rockers in London were the first to liberate poodle skirts from mothballs, and in New York, gal followers of punk-rock fifties enthusiasts the Ramones were devoted to the look. In the early 1980s, circle skirts and bobby sox—this time with high heels instead of saddle shoes—trickled into mainstream teenybop fashion, with popular rockabilly bands such as the Stray Cats driving the point home. Ten years later in the mid-1990s, the poodle saw a small resurgence with a revived interest in "cocktail culture" and swing dancing. Celebrating a less innocent, more-martini-than-Kool-Aid memory of the fifties, women unearthed circle skirts from the basements of thrift stores and morphed them into a sexier, more modern style. Twenty-first-century Japanese anime renewed interest in fashion appliqués with cute 1970s-inspired animal icons. Perhaps Hello Kitty and wide-eyed Bambi can give old-school poodle skirts a postmillennial kick.

"The miniskirt enables young ladies to run faster, and because of it, they may have to."

◇◇◇

JOHN LINDSAY,
New York City mayor (1966–1973)

CHAPTER 12

THE MINISKIRT REVOLUTION

Of the late 1960s miniskirt, this we know: It never would have come to pass without the advent of pantyhose. A radical departure from the previous decade's good-girl petticoat styles, the miniskirt time-traveled to the future while borrowing from the androgynous flappers of the past, driving young women into futuristic wear, including vinyl go-go boots, Pop-Art tights, and thigh-bearing dresses far too short to hide garter belts and stockings. Heavens-soaring hemlines put parents, teachers, and preachers on the offensive: The kids were blissfully out of control.

The 1960s was an era of optimism and prosperity. The Space Race was on, and to the Western world, the future had arrived. Innovation and convenience were buzzwords, and the mass-market ready-to-wear industry was booming, bringing

the cost of clothing down to lower than ever before. A dress that would have cost about $12 in the 1920s might now cost $5.98, thanks to sweatshop labor and hearty, inexpensive man-made textiles, like polyester and rayon. Nineteen sixty-one was also the year of the Pill, heralding a new era of independence for women.

Youth now had prosperity, power, and choices: They wanted to celebrate, and the new fashions were right in step with this groovy, swinging zeitgeist. After fifteen years of the New Look, women were eager to look less like princesses and more liberated and electrifying. In Paris, designer Pierre Cardin launched a line of synthetic space-age outfits for women, and Yves Saint Laurent crafted short, boxy shifts patterned in geometric Mondrian prints. London was the place to be, and King's Road was the epicenter of the scene, where the coolest cats were the mods—a moniker short for modernists.

miniskirt

Sophisticated and stylish, mods wore closely tailored clothes, listened to American R&B, smoked cigarettes in Italian coffee shops, followed the art scene, and bought clothes at the hippest boutique in the 'hood, Bazaar.

It is Bazaar's owner, a fab mod in a five-point bob named Mary Quant, who is generally credited with launching the iconic miniskirt in London in 1965. Inspired by the revolutionary above-the-knee designs introduced the previous year by French designer André Courrèges, Quant one-upped her contemporary and lopped several more inches off the hemlines of her simple A-line dresses. She called these threads minis.

The thigh—that last reasonable bastion of modesty—was exposed. Starting six or seven inches above the knee, Quant's skirts were now shorter than any others in the history of Western women's dress. Almost always cut in an A-line, the skirts were often sewn without a proper waistband and

PANTYHOSE:
A BRIEF HISTORY

Without the advent of pantyhose—tights with full coverage from waist to toes—skirts too short to cover garter clasps may have never reached the masses. Invented by Allen Gant, Sr., in 1959, the first pantyhose had a seam up the back and could be worn with an optional opaque nylon binding, eliminating the need for multiple foundation garments (garters, belts, corsets, and the like). In 1965, the same year the miniskirt was introduced, seamless pantyhose were conceived, creating a smooth leg that was made to look more "natural" in colors like "American Suntan." Bare legs were still a no-no, so the higher hemlines rose, the more those thick, leggings-like tights replaced stockings and became their own fashion statement. Textured with ribs, weaves, fishnets, and loud patterns, legs became the focus of the outfit. Stockings and their accoutrements were all but forgotten—except in the boudoir—until the 1990s when a sexualized fetish look entered the mainstream.

merely finished in a light facing so they "floated" on the hips.
To provide some form of cover, gals donned tights, a denser
offspring of the recently invented pantyhose, woven in bright,
opaque colors or wild psychedelic patterns.

Despite the miniskirt's shockingly short length, the
accompanying dolly-girl look and Op Art styling the mod
chicks adopted gave an overall effect that was far more
saccharine than slutty. Like the flapper, the ideal mod girl
was quite boyish. Supermodel Twiggy was the defining
image of the era; her flat chest, concave hips, and all-angles
limbs formed the coveted figure. And like the mods' posturing
predecessors, stance and attitude were important elements
of the completed look. Angular, awkward, and almost clumsy,
these underfed skeletons championed a geeky-gawky
broken-limb pose, paired with a dumb-blonde doe-eyed
stare and affected, vapid laughter, an ironic mask of their
distinct mindsets.

Minis created a revolution and turned fashion on its
heel. By the late sixties, there were few limits to how daring a
designer could go with a mini. Paco Rabanne introduced
a chain-mail minidress made of tiny disks linked by plastic and
metal. Skirts were made in see-through plastic material, PVC,
and knitted in loose crochet, so colorful panties and bras
became a full-fledged part of the outfit. The micro-miniskirt
was so short you couldn't dare sit down in it. Only about

chain-mail
mini

thirteen inches long and sometimes buttoned up the front,
a girl had to think twice before taking a seat.

In the end, though, fashion may have been unshackled but
women were not necessarily liberated. As restrictive as the
hobble skirt was to legs and walking, so too was the micro-mini:
Smaller steps were necessary to avoid panty flashing; climbing in

and out of cars was an exercise in delicacy; and sports and games were out of the question. And because nothing was left to the imagination, a tough-to-achieve stick-thin figure drove thousands of girls to develop unrealistic body-image issues.

Maybe the death knell of the miniskirt was the eating disorders, or maybe it was the fact that the style became so mainstream that mothers were raiding their daughters' closets, but the short skirts fell out of favor at the end of the decade. In 1970, Gordon Franklin, president of Saks Fifth Avenue, was quoted in *Life* magazine saying, "The mini is dead as a doornail."

The short skirts had a resurgence in the late 1970s, thanks to the punk movement, in a look that married bondage wear with tough-girl 1950s styling. Reincarnated in PVC, black leather, and stretch fabrics, this mini gave the finger to the man—there were no doe-eyed dolly-girls here.

As the 1980s peaked, power women in suits adopted the short skirt. The mini was now not only worn in the office, it was closing deals and calling shots. This version, though still short, was more tailored and made in stretchy fabrics that gave leggy women flexibility and freedom. Baby-doll girls had grown into butt-kicking, assertive business leaders who exchanged Miss and Mrs. for Ms. Through the 1990s and into the twenty-first century, the popularity of the miniskirt hasn't waned. As long as there is a woman with a great set of legs and an even larger sense of self, there will always be an occasion to wear a mini.

PAPER DRESSES

The Space Age launched a number of futuristic fashion fads, but none was as big a craze as the paper dress. The original "Paper Caper" minidress was sold for $1 by the Scott Paper Company in 1966 and came with 52 cents worth of coupons. The colorful A-line frock was to be thrown away after one use—"After all, who is going to do laundry in space?" mused one observer—and Scott sold half a million of the things. Hallmark, Dove, Lux, and Lifebuoy jumped on board and offered their own version of the paper minidress. Campbell's even created the punny "Souper Dress," printed in a pattern of rows of tomato cans, piggybacking on the success of Andy Warhol's Pop-Art paintings. Another company, Paraphernalia, invented a Chia Pet–style paper minidress embedded with flower seeds that apparently blossomed after it was misted. Presidential candidate George Romney made promotional campaign dresses, and graphic designer Harry Gordon created a line covered in rock 'n' roll poster art. Paper clothing stores sprang up across the country (even offering disposable paper swimsuits!) and department stores opened "newsstand" and "waste-paper boutiques" within their ladies departments. Made of cellulose and nylon, the paper minidress was more the consistency of a dried-out Handi Wipe than paper, and could be worn carefully about ten times before getting the heave-ho—providing the wearer avoided the errant lit cigarette butt and didn't get too close to the barbecue at picnics. Alas, after one too many fashionistas went up (literally) in flames, by 1969, the dangerous and wasteful garments were discarded once and for all.

paper dress

"Fashion is born by small facts, trends, or even politics . . . or by the shortening or lengthening of a skirt."

◇◇◇

ELSA SCHIAPARELLI,
shockingly innovative fashion designer

CHAPTER 13

FOLK SONGS AND FLOWER DREAMS

prairie skirts

Conservatives love to cast stones at deadbeats, but if it wasn't for these alienated hooligans, we wouldn't have the darling broomstick skirt today. The broomstick, also known as the prairie, gypsy, or peasant skirt, encapsulates the flower-powerful magic carpet ride better known as the hippie movement of the 1960s. As with many countercultures, most people resent it, despise it, or try to snuff it out before they wake up and cheerfully emulate the very way of life they previously scorned. It was the far-out hippie clothes that mainstream society coveted. Sure, they shunned the draft-dodging, long-haired, dope-smoking dropouts, but they longed for their fabulously frayed and deliciously disheveled outfits. The bell-bottoms! The denim! The hot-pants! And the skirts—the skirts were the best.

Hippie style was a patchwork of homegrown, unkempt anti-fashion—perhaps flowing skirts made for easier access in an era of free love—that rebelled against the prim, coiffed look that dominated most of the 1960s. If King's Road in London was the epicenter of mod fashion in the early part of the decade, the Haight-Ashbury district in San Francisco was ground zero for the hippie movement in the late sixties and early seventies. There, young people embraced the maxim of the time: Turn on, tune in, drop out—in other words, get high, get paranoid, and do nothing. Because of the depressing political climate of the time, what began as a subculture of disenchanted young liberals was soon embraced by much of the mainstream. The kids insisted the Vietnam War was a sham and burned their draft cards, shocking and shaming their parents. Seeking enlightenment beyond what LSD tabs offered, hippies trekked the hashish trail to Bangladesh and Katmandu, learning Buddhism and Hare Krishna mantras, and brought colorfully printed fabrics and native costumes back with them. Some groups even left the cities altogether and moved to rural communes to create utopian agricultural communities and eke out a living sewing hammocks and weaving potholders.

When they weren't wearing their beloved denim, hippie women wore long skirts excavated from secondhand stores, homemade, or brought back from or inspired by

hippie skirt

PRAIRIE-SKIRT SONGWRITERS— FOLK, HIPPIE, AND COUNTRY GREATS

Joni Mitchell
Joan Baez
The Mamas and the Papas
Peter, Paul, and Mary
Judy Collins
Laura Nyro
Emmylou Harris
Stevie Nicks
Loretta Lynn
Dolly Parton

Middle Eastern treks. Loose, flowing, and multitiered in the style of gypsies and belly dancers, prairie skirts reached to the ankle or mid-calf and were patterned in busy prints, tie-dyes, and psychedelic colors. Worn with clogs or leather sandals, T-shirts or peasant blouses, and lots of beaded jewelry, the long skirts projected a look of unbridled idealism that combined eastern European gypsy and Far East enlighten-ment with American Indian and colonial pioneer naturalism.

Finger-on-the-pulse fashion designers couldn't help but take notice of this growing trend and crafted their own watered-down versions of bohemia. Their designs enhanced all the romance and embellishment of hippie clothes and ignored the predominant DIY aspect of the style. With the help of designers like Christian Dior, Zandra Rhodes, and the London fashion boutique Biba, prairie skirts made their way from the commune to the catwalk. In 1968, Giorgio Sant'Angelo piled multicolored ruffled skirts atop one another, and another designer named Mollie Parnis went as far as teaming flounced gypsy skirts with a jeweled bra and a demure ruffled bolero. In 1969, Christian Dior presented a bohemian-chic inspired collection of colorful gypsy-style silk party dresses and skirts made of patchworks of patterns and ruffled tiers, and Yves Saint Laurent's Marrakesh-inspired couture incorporated lush, rippling velvets and printed silks. Laura Ashley was a struggling British fashion house when it forayed into prairie skirts. The designs not only put the company on the map but, by 1970, launched a country-kitchen empire.

In the early 1970s, Joni Mitchell and Joan Baez were the poster children for commune-chic, and every little girl wanted long ironed hair and a ruffled skirt. In 1973, the Japanese designer Kenzo kept the look alive with a collection of youthful pleated skirts he called broomstick skirts, after the traditional folk method used, where a tiered prairie skirt was wrapped around a broomstick, dyed and dried, rendering it pleated and wrinkled. In 1976, the tiered skirt got another gasp in collections from Anne Klein and Donna Karan, who insisted that New World peasantry was the future of fashion.

Around this same time, folk dancing experienced a big revival in the U.S., and the popular costume of the set

broomstick skirt

included an abbreviated version of the prairie skirt, made girlishly poufy with petticoats. Alas, with these new nerdy associations—and the rising ultra-glam disco style—the prairie skirt was not long for this world. Once pants and jeans became the favored uniform, the poor skirts went down in popularity. Soon, prairies were linked primarily with Goody Two-shoes and Laura Ashley's tiresome calico prints. Hippie hangers-on still wore them, though, and in the mid 1980s when the Grateful Dead found themselves on top of the music charts with an unlikely hit record—their very first—college campuses witnessed a brief sixties-style crinkled prairie skirt resurgence.

After years at the bottom of the fashion caste system, in 2004 the prairie skirt reappeared out of nowhere in a boho-chic style, and was rechristened the broomstick. By the summer of 2005, it seemed that every woman had one, not only on the street but in evening wear, too. Monique Lhuillier, for one, introduced a fall line that included floor-sweeping, three-tiered ballgown broomstick skirts in jewel-tone silks. Right in step, designers like Donna Karan, Giorgio Armani, Marc Jacobs, Prada, and Marni created their own versions of the prairie. Worn with cowboy boots or flip-flops, halter tops, and wooden or turquoise jewelry, the broomstick tied together a savvy, laidback look that would make Ali MacGraw proud.

"Say what you
want about long dresses,
but they cover a
multitude of shins."

◇◇◇

MAE WEST,
brash, sexy film star

CHAPTER 14

PRE-DISCO DOLDRUMS

the mini-midi-maxi debate

The greatest thing the miniskirt did for skirt fashion was break the hemline barrier, and from that moment on the *wearer* dictated the length she wanted to wear, not what designers deemed chic for the season. Skirt fans took that freedom to the nth degree. Through the sixties several options were available, and the mini—as well as the micro-mini— were sharing closet space with a little nugget called the midi and a longer piece called the maxi.

The miniskirt was popular through the decade (rain and snow be damned), but not everyone rode the bandwagon. As early as spring of 1967—just two years after the mini's debut—*Time* magazine declared, "Now that the miniskirt is being sported eight inches above the knee, it is apparent

maxi
skirt

midi
skirt

that the only possible direction for hemlines is down." The same season, Brit designer and one-time mini enthusiast Ossie Clarke warned, "This summer will be one last fling to show your legs. Next year the idea will be to wrap 'em up warm."

By the fall of 1967, French ready-to-wear designers Daniel Hechter and Jacques Delahaye introduced "maxi jupes" just as longer skirts from Clarke and Roland Klein hit the runways. The just-below-the-knee, often A-line skirts—zipped or buttoned in the back or on the side, or elastic-waisted—were a practical but staid style that offered a work-and-wind-friendly alternative to the foot-long mini. Quickly dubbed "midis," the new design joined the mini on fashion racks—proving that Clarke's prediction was premature and that hell had frozen over: Fashionable women had hemline choices beyond only what designers and fashion editors dictated.

it's a drag

While suburbia frolicked between minis and midis, chic urban women sought a bad-girl outlet, but what would it be? The mini had already set the bar shockingly high, and the midi was too square, so where could hemlines go? In a bit of reverse psychology, elongating the skirt even more than the midi became the rage as an ironic fashion statement. Hemlines dropped all the way to the floor, marking the longest skirt length since 1914. Initially pooh-poohed when first introduced as street wear in 1969—floor-length dresses had been worn as evening wear for decades—the maxiskirt, an ankle-to-floor-length, often garishly patterned A-line skirt, was soon trapping dust bunnies, collecting twigs, and pushing other rubbish across the floors of the Western world.

Usually made of heavier material like wool or cotton and sometimes even quilted, the maxiskirt used heavy batting to keep the hemline weighted down. And what did women wear with the maxiskirt? Maxi coats, of course, paired with trailing mufflers and scarves long enough to wrap around a buffalo. Tall gals benefited most from this look, while shorter fashion victims risked being mistaken for walking sleeping bags.

Burdened down by so much fabric, the maxi look fell on the sloppy side of chic. But try and tell that to the legions of fashion-conscious women in the Midwest and other cold-weather areas who vowed to never bare leg through another winter again. The plummeting skirt length also coincided with a revival of hairy legs on equality-seeking women who asked, If men aren't shaving gam, why should we?

As the new decade broke, seriously different lengths of the classic A-line skirt were now available. Mini, midi, maxi—it was a seventies-era Latin fashion mantra for *I wore it, I won't wear it, I'll never wear it again!* The three styles drove fashion editors crazy. Confused writers offered a pell-mell of reviews, declaring the maxi a homely disgrace, a knockout, then dead, alive, and finally dead again. Fashion magazines normally lectured readers with a sniff of authority, scolding women who would dare sway from the mode manifesto. But editors soon caved to the idea that perhaps women could decide for themselves which skirt best suited their figures, and lightened up just a little bit on the rules. *Women's Wear Daily* publisher John Fairchild shrugged, saying, "The wheels keep turning and fashion goes from long to short and short to long." Rather than absolute dos and don'ts, the 1970s offered a big bag of *please-dos*!

So why did fashion editors finally acknowledge all those skirt lengths after centuries of one-length-fits-all? The social climate, for one thing, was as volatile as hemlines. The closing years of the 1960s were a time of both idealism and despondency. Great movements—the civil rights, antiwar, and women's lib—were on the front lines, battling for freedom, peace, and equality. As the future looked less stable, fashion became slightly nostalgic (long hemlines) as well as rebellious (short hemlines), and experimental styles strived to fit outside the too-square box called the Establishment. Skirts were just doing their best to keep up.

The maxiskirt was worn for about four years, but it had its detractors, be sure of that. Of the floor-length style, Jack Hanson, founder of California's chi-chi Jax boutiques, sneered, "It's like admitting you don't have good legs." One anonymous male observer offered *Time* magazine this gem: "I don't mind

HOLLYWOOD MOMENTS:
FAMOUS SKIRTS IN FILMS

There are two end-all moments in the movies that encapsulate the allure and power of the skirt: Marilyn Monroe in *The Seven Year Itch*, standing over a breezy subway grate as her white pleated skirt blows up around her shoulders, and the too-revealing interrogation scene in *Basic Instinct*, during which a panty-free Sharon Stone famously crosses and uncrosses her legs in a tight micro-miniskirt. But many other skirts deserve props for their less iconic but just as memorable moments on the silver screen.

- In Laurel and Hardy's *Putting Pants on Philip* (1927), whenever Stan—in a Scottish kilt—sees a good-looking woman he does a scissors kick and takes off in pursuit. Predating Marilyn, a blast of air from a sidewalk grate lifts Stan's kilt, causing several young women to faint.
- Claudette Colbert one-ups Clark Gable and hitches up her below-the-knee straight skirt to catch a ride in *It Happened One Night* (1934), quipping, "I proved once and for all that the limb is mightier than the thumb."
- Jane Fonda's interstellar plastic and vinyl micro-miniskirts in *Barbarella* (1968) didn't even try to cover the space cadet's girlish white panties.
- Faye Dunaway shooting pictures on the streets of New York in a glamorous Yves Saint Laurent split skirt in *Eyes of Laura Mars* (1978).
- Then unknown Helen Hunt's schoolgirl-cool reversible skirt—

leather mini on one side, Catholic school uniform on the other—in *Girls Just Want to Have Fun* (1985).

- In *Pride and Prejudice*—pick your favorite version— Elizabeth Bennett walks across the moors to see her ailing sister and is held in contempt for her muddy skirt hem.
- Patricia Tallman spends the first half of *Night of the Living Dead* (1970) kicking zombie ass in a matronly brown-plaid midi, before changing into army fatigues to do some serious damage.
- On the small screen, nearly every episode of *Ally McBeal* and her micro-miniskirts warrant a nod, especially "It's My Party," in which the diminutive lawyer is held in contempt of court and tossed in jail because her skirt is too short.
- In *Bridget Jones's Diary* (2001), Renee Zellweger, as Bridget, launched an affair with Hugh Grant, who played her boss, Daniel, by wearing an impossibly short skirt to the office. Daniel commented via e-mail, "You appear to have forgotten your skirt. Is skirt off sick?" Bridget flirted back, "Skirt is demonstrably neither sick nor absent. Appalled by management's blatantly size-ist attitude to skirt. Suggest management sick, not skirt."
- In *Transamerica* (2005), Felicity Huffman delicately lifts her midi to pee, revealing that she is a woman playing a man becoming a woman.
- Lastly, we should not leave out our skirt-sporting leading men, including Cary Grant in *I Was a Male War Bride*, Tony Curtis and Jack Lemmon in *Some Like It Hot*, Dustin Hoffman in *Tootsie*, Anthony Perkins in the last scene of *Psycho*, Michael Caine in *Dressed to Kill*, and almost every episode of *Monty Python*.

a long coat if it is handsome and the girl in it is Geraldine Chaplin, like in *Doctor Zhivago*, but underneath I like to find Julie Christie, in this year's mini." Naturally.

Older women in particular *loathed* the long lengths, which in Paris were called "young lengths," because only the youthful could wear them without seeming dowdy. Anything knee-length and above was dubbed the "mature look" because older women couldn't get enough of them—they felt the style shaved years off their age.

With its characteristic crazy-quilt fabrics and leaf-raking length, the maxiskirt is an easy target to dis, but it wasn't all frump—this was the era of free love and bra burning. Pair the modest maxi with a tight T-shirt sans bra, groupie-girl platform clogs, big sunglasses, and a hobo bag, and it was very seventies-era confident-smart sexy. And who can argue with that?

Meanwhile, like the best romances, the midi was fated to endure a love-hate-love-loathe relationship with gals of all ages. In the August 21, 1970, edition of *Life* magazine, a cover story, "The Midi Muscles In," trumpeted: "Farewell to knees and maybe even calves if the anti-mini forces have their way." Barbara Walters loved the midi and often paired it with tall boots for *The Today Show*. Said she, "Like it or not, I'm seen by more people than any other woman in this country, and when I wear a midi, that's it." Doris Day also loved wearing midis, while *All My Children*'s (and, later, *Saturday Night Fever* hoofer) Karen Lynn

Gorney protested it, saying, "The straight ones with the slit up the front make you look just like a French whore, they really do!" Four years later, in 1974, the *New York Times* referred to the midi phenomenon as "a fiasco," and commented that most women "quite violently" opposed the lengths. (Apparently, hell hath no fury like a woman adorned in an unflattering skirt.)

But the midi, in various shapes and cuts, has been here to stay all the same. Though no longer called the midi, knee-length and below-the-knee-length A-line skirts have proven a comfortable and stylish length for the generations of assertive women since the late 1960s, and one can always find evidence of it on store racks somewhere, or at the least, chafing the hips of polyester-clad waitresses at Bob's Big Boys the countryside over.

The maxi, quite frankly, has seen better days. Excluding a few minor comebacks in severe, unflattering cuts, the maxi as street wear never made another splash as big as when it did at the turn of the 1970s. But in the spring of 2006, the maxiskirt made its first appearance in nearly thirty years, looking remarkably similar to its 1970s ancestor. Brightly patterned, loose and flowing, the modern floor-length A-line maxi is an extension of the boho-chic look that dominated a segment of high fashion in the first years of the 2000s—minus hairy legs and the absence of bras. Those are two retro trends that twenty-first-century women haven't re-embraced—yet.

"There is one standard
for people, and there is another
standard for 'skirts'."

◇◇◇

ANNA QUINDLEN,
Pulitzer Prize–winning author and journalist

CHAPTER 15

THE SEXLESS TROUSER SKIRT

hear me roar

In 1973, women were entrenched in the debate about whether they should continue as housewives or tackle the feminist thing and bring home the bacon. For the earnest gal who wanted to work and be taken seriously—a novel concept in 1973—there was the bleak trouser skirt, available in gay shades of brown and olive or a drab plaid. No wonder staying home in a bathrobe still held appeal!

Despite the fact that slacks had become acceptable garments for women in the 1960s, and ladies' trousers and jeans were *de rigueur* by the 1970s, society could not come to terms with women wearing any kind of trouser in the workplace. Pants were considered professional for men but highly inappropriate for women. Never mind the fact that five years earlier, business owners had caved with lightning speed to accommodate miniskirts for bank tellers, secretaries, and other female-dominated careers—pants just wouldn't do. As women continued to advance in the male-dominated workforce, men—they called all the shots in those days—scratched their heads over what they should "allow" women to wear. In 1969, for instance, women in ROTC groups on college campuses were assigned "female" versions of men's uniforms and, apparently untroubled by the irony, wore straight skirts with low-heeled pumps and stockings to gun-drill sessions on the lawn.

Around that time, the midi skirt was gradually modified to mirror the look of trousers. Shaped in a relaxed A-line or

trouser skirt

narrow and tight with a back kick pleat (an inverted pleat that allowed a bit of movement), the high-rise waistline featured a front fly and fastener and one or two pockets in front and sometimes one or two pockets on the bum. It came just below the knee or, in some cases, to mid-calf.

The uniform-style, straight-shaped trouser skirt gave women all the blandness of slacks but with none of the ease—straight skirts limited stride length—promising a meet-you-somewhere-in-the-middle compromise with the ever-more popular pair of pants.

"Isn't it great to feel all-girl again?" cried a 1972 ad from Macy's about the merits of polyester trouser skirts. "Show off long legs in a new type of skirt-classic that borrows the best in tailored fit from your favorite trousers." Tailored, yes. Attractive? That part was questionable.

The trouser skirt wasn't really a couture designer kind of thing. It was more of a discount department store kind of thing. Stitched in synthetics, all-wool fabrics, tweeds, corduroy, or cotton twill, little effort was made to sauce the thing up. Why not add invisible zippers, for instance, or cheerful patterns? The purpose of the trouser skirt was to look smart, utilitarian, classic—but most important, as androgynous as an unbifurcated garment can allow. Wearing the trouser skirt assured women they could work alongside—and in most cases, beneath—men, in a nonthreatening, nonsuggestive, unfeminine-yet-leggy skirt.

SKIRTING THE LAW

Who knew skirts could cause so much trouble? Even in the twenty-first century, women (and, in some cases, men) found the simple garment delivered more than its wearer intended. Some notable cases include:

- In the 1960s, entire nations, including Madagascar, Swaziland, and Malawi, outlawed the miniskirt.
- Provocative dressing may lead to sexual harassment, wrote Chief Justice William H. Rehnquist in 1986 for Meritor Savings Bank v. Vinson, in which a woman who wore a skirt was repeatedly raped by a male supervisor. Skirt-wearing discrimination aside, the Supreme Court ruled in favor of the victim anyway.
- Lehman v. Toys "R" Us was a landmark case of 1993, in which the Supreme Court not only ruled in favor of an employee who had her skirt lifted and was degraded by a coworker but redefined what constitutes a hostile work environment.
- In 1999, King County, Washington, Superior Court Judge Jeanette Burrage barred female lawyers from wearing pantsuits in her courtroom, demanding they dress more "professionally"—in skirts. The Seattle battle-ax lost her next election, the "skirt issue" being a primary concern working against her.
- In 2001, a British investment banker settled out of court against her former employer after quitting a job where she was asked to wear only short skirts, among a host of other vile requests.
- The miniskirt was prohibited in Swaziland until 1969 for morality reasons, and once again outlawed in schools in 2000

because it was believed it would help prevent the spread of AIDS. The ban was lifted, but in 2004 city bus drivers announced they would rape any female passenger seen wearing a miniskirt, saying, "They want to be raped, and we're giving them what they want."

- In Washington State in 2002, it was deemed illegal to film up women's skirts without their permission.
- In 2004, a Santa Ana judge admonished a pregnant female attorney for wearing pants in the courtroom, saying her appearance "leaves a lot to be desired."
- In January of 2006, a male New Jersey high school student won the right to wear a skirt to school.
- According to one ten-year-old Pennsylvania girl, wearing miniskirts to school is an inalienable right, and in April 2006 she challenged her elementary school principal, who insisted girls' skirts at her school must fall below the knees. The plucky tween organized a protest carrying a sign reading: STYLE IS FREEDOM.
- In April 2006, sixty-four-year-old deputy president Jacob Zuma, the leading government official responsible for women's rights and the effort against AIDS—and perhaps the most popular politician in the African National Congress—was arrested for allegedly raping a thirty-one-year-old anti-AIDS advocate. Zuma claimed the woman had signaled a desire to have sex with him by wearing a knee-length skirt to his house and sitting with her legs crossed, revealing her thigh. His accuser was clearly aroused, he said, and "in the Zulu culture, you cannot just leave a woman if she is ready." To deny her sex, he said, would have been tantamount to rape. A month later, he was acquitted.
- The Houston Bar Association's dress code still requires female attorneys to wear skirts to work.

skirts of fury

Now here's the rub: In their trouser skirts, women were decked out as acceptably attired camp counselors, postal workers, secretaries, and meter maids, and they sashayed into the workforce, greeted by an environment that was quite hostile toward them. Sexual harassment was rampant, and throughout the 1970s, women did what they had almost always done—kept a stiff upper lip—while getting groped, felt up, and degraded in their leg-baring skirts. Turns out, creeps will hit on women in unflattering skirts as much as they will hit on those in pretty ones.

By the 1980s, the balance of power still leaned heavily in favor of men, but women had gained a little leverage. Men were *slowly* learning how to work alongside women in a sensitive and respectful manner—though there was much room for improvement. Encouraged by their newfound influence in the workplace, many skirt-wearing women theorized that short hemlines equaled empowerment, allowing both freedom of movement and freedom to choose how to dress. Women in power felt it was their right to wear a short skirt, and if a man took the display of leg as a come-on, that was his problem. In 1987, designers such as Emanuel Ungaro, Michael Kors, Isaac Mizrahi, and Donna Karan jumped to accommodate these working girls, creating business suits with shockingly short and tight miniskirts. Excepting certain

1980s
miniskirt

SKORTS TO SKANTS

Some women can commit to a skirt; others have to ease into the idea. Hence the invention of skorts, a combination of skirt and shorts, and the inverse mullets of the skirt world, with the party in the front and business in the back. Usually made of stretch or regular cotton, the wishy-washy design is essentially a pair of utilitarian shorts with an apron-like front and the backside revealing the bifurcated shorts. The design is a derivative of culottes, a split or divided knee-length skirt, fuller at the bottom hem than at the waist, created in the late nineteenth century to provide more freedom for women to do activities like gardening, bike riding, and still look like they're wearing a skirt. The look was updated for women in the military; from 1951 to 1971, enlisted women wore a taupe three-piece exercise suit consisting of a cotton chambray shirt and denim cloth skort, which the military called a divided skirt. A later style was worn with white tennis shoes and cotton taupe anklets for fatigue duties, physical training, and sports activities. The skort made a big comeback with regular gals in the mid-1990s, before women realized that a skirt is a skirt and shorts are shorts, and the skort went scarce.

In 1999, the skant, a skirt-pants combination, appeared in stores. Ankle-length or knee-length boot-cut pants had material fastened with a kilt-like front buckle or buttons. Very few people bought it, and the style was only around for about a year. Shortly after, women began wearing skirts over pants, in a laid-back look that mixed slovenly with tailored. Lacy silk skirts over jeans or knee-length tweeds over slacks, no skirt-and-pant combination was too diverse for the hobo-chic gal.

conservative professions, the trouser skirt became an antiquated ideal of professionalism and was tossed aside for the ever-rising, office-friendly miniskirt.

Today the trouser skirt is pretty much delegated solely to those whose work requires a uniform—and even then women are often given the option of pants or, in some blessed cases, Bermuda shorts. In these professions, such as the military, some women still get flak for choosing to wear pants on occasions where a skirt might be more appropriate. To wear a skirt, to not wear a skirt—the scrap of a garment has become an unlikely, and adorable, feminist symbol.

skort

"Fashion is what
you adopt when you don't
know who you are."

◇◇◇

QUENTIN CRISP,
English writer, actor, and consummate raconteur

CHAPTER 16

THE TWENTY-FIRST CENTURY

anti-fashion and avant-garde

The 1980s was a decade of excess, and fashion designers pushed construction and design to the hilt, creating asymmetrical, outrageously pleated, and dramatically cut skirts that were as architectural as they were fashionable. Yet as avant-garde as designers went, their creations often hearkened back to older styles from yesteryear.

The advent of MTV made huge contributions to fashion and brought punk and new wave into the mainstream. Musicians now had a twenty-four-hour stage, and the world watched and copied them. Most skirts of that era were pure performance—Cyndi Lauper wore a newspaper-fringed flying-saucer skirt, and the B-52s' matching miniskirts were hemmed with hula hoops. But, as with the subculture prairie

flying-saucer
skirts

skirts before them, the theatrical inspiration trickled down
into mainstream costume. In 1985, Vivienne Westwood,
whose clothes seemed to single-handedly dress everyone in
Britain's new wave scene, introduced her mini-crini, impossibly tiny ruffled skirts supported by collapsible hoops and
equally diminutive nineteenth-century petticoats. The skirt
was extensively copied, as was Christian Lacroix's famous
pouf skirt, widely worn by young leggy girls. At first deemed
too unflattering to catch on—the skirts were literally large,
poufy pods, dropping from the waist and gathering up above
the knees—the style was popularized in formal wear, right
down to Middle America's high-school prom dresses.

pouf skirt

asymetric skirt

The decade was a playground of fashion, underscoring Andy Warhol's statement that "Art is anything you can get away with," and most designers did. Like a mad scientist running tests in a laboratory, Issey Miyake hit his stride in the eighties and began experimenting with new natural and synthetic materials, mixing and superimposing them on one another, pleating, twisting, bleaching, quilting, knitting, crumpling, and recycling, to build strange pleats, shapes, and proportions. His skirts were works of architecture and changed contemporary notions of fit and proportion.

Not content to flatter women's figures, Rei Kawakubo of Comme des Garçons and Yohji Yamamoto cloaked bodies beneath dark, luminous geometric shapes and practiced exacting irregularity, asymmetry, and imperfection. Skirts were slashed, knotted or tied up, and draped in designs often referred to as "post-nuclear bag-lady." Yamamoto's little black dress of 1986 featured a skirt with a shocking, nineteenth-century-inspired scarlet tulle bustle cascading from the backside and down to the floor. Neither conventionally feminine nor traditionally decorative, the nonfunctional quality initially appalled the press, but "the Japanese look," as his baggy, sack-like shapes were referred to, was embraced by influential—and visible—customers such as the Thompson Twins and Bananarama, and oversized, irregularly cut skirts became art-chick chic.

bandage skirt

In the latter eighties and early nineties, Azzedine Alaïa worked with acetate and knit and made full-length, perfect-fit bandage skirts that were slashed, tucked, and knotted. These hugged the body from waist to ankle, lifting hips and molding legs to create a modern, more functional update on the hobble skirt. A very tall, model-thin figure was essential for wearing his clothes well, and indeed, the glamazon models of that era were some of Alaïa's biggest fans.

Gianni Versace's Bondage collection of 1992 glorified sexual fetishes and featured floor-length leather-and-chain ball-gown skirts paired with leather bras.

bondage skirt

The avant-garde of the new millennium was pioneered by a fresh crop of bad boys and girls. In 2001, Junya Watanabe of Comme des Garçons made a Tweety Bird–yellow skirt that looked like a crepe-paper sculpture blended with cotton candy; other Watanabe skirts were striped with double-ruffle irregular hemlines and conjured nineteenth-century French circus performers. The work of Hussein Chalayan was particularly striking: His skirts were heavily deconstructed, with sections cut out and replaced, seams left visible, and hemlines on a single skirt varying in length. His "Tulle Dress Before Minis Now 2000" line featured a confectionary dream of a skirt that looked like bunches of marzipan flowers. Like many of their peers, these designers were creating works of art as worthy of a gallery exhibition as a walk down the runway.

Of course, real gals aren't strutting down Main Street in skirts encircled in stuffed velvet tubing, as models did for Chalayan's spring 2006 collection. But asymmetrical and frayed hemlines were quickly accepted as fashionable detailing. With these artists at the helm of the new millennium, we can bet that mainstream skirts morph into riskier and more whimsical shapes and designs. The theme of the twenty-first century is "anything goes," and designers will continue to rework the tried and true, combining classic shapes with modern inspirations.

deconstructed
skirt

"Fashion is architecture. It is a matter of proportion."

◇◇◇

COCO CHANEL,
trendsetting Parisian fashion pioneer

CHAPTER 17

THE THIGH'S THE LIMIT

the low-rise

Just when we thought the thigh was the limit, skirts found new skin to expose. The low-rise micro-miniskirt, a.k.a. the Band-Aid or the Belt, plunged to new depths, this time from above and below. Not only did the hemline rise to meet the panty line, but the waistline sunk below the hip bone.

how low can they go?

First spotted on celebrants at such venerable fashion trendsetting institutions as the annual Sturgis Motorcycle Rally in North Dakota and the Frederick's of Hollywood catalog, the impossible low-rise is not for the faint of heart. A favorite of biker chicks, girls gone wild, and happy hookers, the low-rise parties in both the front *and* the back, baring hip bone and a bit of ass cheek. A stick-thin figure—not to mention a Brazilian

low-rise
micro
miniskirt

bikini wax—is essential to wearing the low-rise as it gravitates toward fat and rolls up at the touch of it. Usually crafted out of any stretch material, this ultra-mini tends not to employ print fabrics—there's really no room for patterns—and is best worn with G-string underwear, which serves as a sort of an anchor to keep the scrap in place. Some gals even eschew undergarments altogether, making the skirt both outer and underwear.

The low-rise has its origins with, of course, the miniskirt of the 1960s but also with the glam and punk movements, two phenomena that used shock tactics to draw attention to the unmentionable and ignored. Then in the 1990s, designers Thierry Mugler and Vivienne Westwood, she of mini-crini fame, pushed the boundaries once again and put skirts so short on the catwalk that panties hung below the hemline.

panty-baring
short skirt

Released free to roam the street, you'd think the low-rise skirt would be most appropriate at the Adult Video News Awards, but leave it to Pamela Anderson to bring butt-cheek to the red carpet, wearing a ripped ribbon of denim to the 2001 *Vanity Fair* Academy Awards after-party. Paired with a see-through braless white dress shirt tied Daisy Duke–style at the waist, Anderson's outfit made headlines. Soon after, the low-rise was a fashion staple for the Hollywood party-girl set. By 2004, the *New York Times* gave a shout-out to the sexy low-rise miniskirt as the primary reason for a spike in spring clothing sales.

Where punk had wit and personality, the low-rise micro-miniskirt can only draw attention to (on a good day) flabby ass cheeks and cellulite-dappled tummies, and (on a bad day) bona-fide crotch. Naturally, these are features that don't stop teenagers with hearty appetites from wearing the skirt, expanding the fabric into new and unsettling proportions. The thing is, no one looks good in a low-rise skirt—not outside the bedroom anyway. But with the rising climes of global warming, *Girls Gone Wild,* and other examples of media-hungry flamboyance, there's no telling if the low-rise is here to stay. Suddenly, the hobble skirt doesn't look so bad after all.

BELLY DANCERS, HULA GIRLS, AND THE ORIGINAL LOW-SLUNG SKIRTS

Low-rise everything has its roots in belly dancing, which most experts agree is the world's oldest form of dance. With evidence seen in all ancient cultures, from the Far East to the Middle East, this dance by women for women—no, it was never intended for men—helped prep young ladies for fertility rites and marriage.

Because the nature of belly dancing comes from an impossibly deft torso and hips, a low-slung skirt with the belly exposed is the ideal garment for it. Filmy, brightly colorful flowing skirts (or sometimes pants) in silk or cotton are embellished with beads, coins, and detailed fabric prints.

Belly dancing didn't arrive in the United States until dancer Little Egypt performed a particularly sexy number at the Chicago World's Fair in 1893. Spectators couldn't take their eyes off her exotic rhythms, and belly dancing was soon recorded on film and became a popular subject for silent movies. The costumes and dancing styles were given a Hollywood flair with veils and other props, evolving the art form to a new level. These days, women have reclaimed belly dancing as a cultural dance—and great exercise.

Another folk dance that fascinates is the hula, a Hawaiian form of narrative dancing that focuses on the hands more than the belly. Men and women wear *pa`u*, belly-baring sarongs of painted and embellished pounded mulberry bark, secured at the hip and leaving the breasts bare. The skirts are usually about four yards long, a yard wide, and very thick. Today hula dancers put on shows for tourists wearing less expensive grass skirts, bra-like tops, and mountains of flowered leis, but they still have the same charm as the *pa`u*.

"What a strange power there is in clothing."

◇◇◇

ISAAC BASHEVIS SINGER,
Nobel Prize–winning author

WRAPPING THINGS UP

Through the years, skirts have been liberating and restricting, inspiring and exasperating, but always conversational and, often, quite fabulous. Skirts transcend mere fashion, serving as barometers of the cultural, social, and sexual zeitgeist.

One thing has never wavered, and that is the passion the garment incites as it morphs from one style to the next. In the twentieth century, in which the bulk of historical information archived in newspapers, magazines, and journals is most readily available, it is fascinating to read how hemline lengths incensed the public, fashion editors, and journalists. New skirt styles would often dictate new roles for women to play, and too often the images were not progressive ones. But fashion finallly won that round, and today women have so many choices, so not adopting one skirt style won't make or break a fashionista's reputation. The evolution of skirts safely moved beyond the whims of fashion designers—who are often male and couldn't give a hoot for comfort, practicality, or how critically appearance affects gender roles—and into the hands of the people who wear them: women, who today earn their own money, giving them the ultimate power to dictate what they put on.

It's true that in the twenty-first century, the objectification of women in skirts sadly remains. (The 2004 reports of bus drivers in South Africa issuing statements that they would rape any woman they see on their bus in a miniskirt are particularly grotesque.) Every day women are still judged by their choices of skirt, and the sharp eyes of fashion police are increasingly more critical than ever before.

Yet skirts persevere, despite feedback that ranges from threatening to juvenile to appreciative. Independent and liberated twenty-first-century women have developed the confidence—and paychecks—to look beyond the pages of fashion magazines, developing individualized styles realized by a wide range of skirts. In the past three decades, the idea of pants as a suitable option for women has been accepted nearly worldwide, and yet flippy skirts hold new heights of popularity, with 2005 even heralded by some fashion editors as the "Year of the Skirt."

Happily, the future shows no sign of abandoning this versatile, sexy, and downright cute piece of clothing. If anything, it is more celebrated than ever. Women make no bones about enjoying all of its assets—there's a skirt for all moods, occasions, and personality types. Now that women have the consumer power to dictate which direction skirts will go, we can only imagine that the skirt's evolution will continue to enthrall, enrage, and inspire.

ACKNOWLEDGMENTS

Many terrific resources were extremely useful in writing this book, especially *The Complete History of Costume and Fashion* by Bronwyn Cosgrave, *Key Moments in Fashion: The Evolution of Style* by Nigel Cawthorne, and the historical archives of the *New York Times*, *Time* and *Life* magazines, *Common Threads: A Parade of American Clothing* by Lee Hall, *Changing Appearances: Understanding Dress in Contemporary Society* by George B. Sproles and Leslie Davis Burns, *Costume Reference (1939–1950)* by Marion Sichel, *Survey of Historic Costume* by Phyllis Tortora and Keith Eubank, *History of Men's Costume* by Marion Sichel, and *Decades of Fashion* by Harriet Worsley.

I'd also like to thank editors Kate Perry and Joelle Yudin for their invaluable tips and advice, illustrator Leela Corman, designer Megan Noller Holt, writing gurus Rachel Hart and Lisa Wogan, my big sister and inspiration Shenna Basye Cara, and my mom, Martha Eberle, who can do it all—and look fabulous—in a skirt. Dozens of friends and family members contributed their skirt ideas, memories, and support in the writing of this book. Thanks to you all!